WA
INNE

Skye

pocket mountains

The author and publisher have made every effort to ensure that the information in this publication is accurate, and accept no responsibility whatsoever for any loss, injury or inconvenience experienced by any person or persons whilst using this book.

For the Rhenigidale Ramblers – Fiona, Kirsty, Mara, Poppy and Sandie

published by

pocket mountains ltd

The Old Church, Annanside,
Moffat, Dumfries & Galloway DG10 9HB
www.pocketmountains.com

ISBN: 978-1-916739-10-9

Printed by J Thomson Colour Printers, Glasgow

Introduction

Visitors from all over the world are drawn to Skye's magnificent, distinctive landscapes and the promise of some of the finest walking Scotland has to offer. The island's mountains are revered by experienced hillwalkers, climbers and mountaineers, not least the jagged basalt and gabbro peaks of the Black Cuillin – an awe-inspiring spectacle, towering over the surrounding moors, lochs and glens of Minginish. For walkers with more modest ambitions, Skye also has an abundance of fine hillcountry outwith the Cuillin Hills, as well as some of Britain's most dramatic coastline – providing for numerous walks of varied length and difficulty, making the island something of a walkers' paradise.

The 25 walks included in this guide reflect the range of Skye's diverse landscapes, and all areas of the island, as well as neighbouring Raasay, are covered. The walks are also chosen for opportunities to experience the wildlife and natural history, and to explore the physical traces of island history. These routes vary from relatively short undemanding strolls and half-day walks on coast, moorland and hill to strenuous day-long excursions involving some demanding terrain.

Some of the routes are well-trodden hikes, such as the more accessible summits of the Red Hills and the Cuillin outliers, or the often extremely busy walks around Trotternish's ever-popular Quiraing and Storr Sanctuary – although options are included to extend these routes to less-visited adjacent hilltops. Other walks featured here are relatively unfrequented, including the hills of Kylerhea in the island's eastern extremity, the abandoned village of Dalavil in the Sleat peninsula and the long, tough route along the remarkable Duirinish coast.

The Isle of Skye is the largest island in the Inner Hebrides and the second-largest Scottish island after Lewis and Harris, at 77km long and between 5km and 40km wide with an area of more than 1600 sq km. The coastline of Skye is a series of peninsulas, bays and sea lochs and this is reflected in its Gaelic name An t-Eilean Sgitheanach, or 'the Winged Isle'. Skye's wing-like peninsulas radiate from a mountainous centre dominated by the Cuillin Hills, which form some of the most dramatic mountain scenery in the British Isles.

Skye's distinctive character is born of the particularity of its geography and the specific, sometimes turbulent, history of its settlement, land use and ownership. The physical traces of this history are scattered throughout the island, often still part of the fabric of present-day communities. Indeed, farming, crofting and fishing remain a visible reminder of centuries of continuity amid the townships even if the means and methods have changed over time.

Skye is a relatively populous, thriving island and as its economy has diversified, communities continue to see the ebb and flow of young people leaving and incomers arriving. Skye's essential qualities remain constant, however, and a strong sense of community and cultural identity pervades the island. Nearly half the resident population of around 10,000 are Gaelic speakers and religious observance remains common.

The island's landscapes are extremely varied. Each of the peninsulas has its own distinguishing physical character; the lochan-speckled moorland of Sleat contrasts with the rugged hillcountry and spectacular glens of Minginish, the high coastal cliffs of Duirinish, the sinuous mountain ridges and ancient landslips of Trotternish, the deep incursions of sea lochs and a coastline punctuated with islands, skerries, bays and inlets. Wildlife is everywhere abundant along the coast, out on the moorland, among the hills and up in the sky. Wherever you walk in Skye, history is present in the landscape. Although there are few remaining physical traces of Neolithic settlement, the ruins of Bronze Age and Iron Age structures, including hillforts, duns and brochs, are scattered throughout the island. While the provenance of ancient piles of stones might not always be apparent, the vestiges of more recent past lives are often obvious, particularly the poignant stone ruins of abandoned villages, many of which were purged of their inhabitants during the 19th-century Clearances.

When to go

Spring through to early autumn generally features some spells of good weather and longer days expand the opportunities for getting out and about to explore the island. May and June, in particular, can often be dry and sunny. However, there is also much to recommend visiting in autumn and even in winter for robust walkers with good waterproofs and a positive outlook. In winter, the ever-changing sky and some bracing weather can bring out the elemental best in the island. Unsurprisingly, Skye is considerably quieter outside the main tourist season with the tailing-off of visitor numbers and holiday traffic.

Weather

At times the weather on Scotland's Atlantic seaboard can be challenging with high winds and persistent rain a year-round possibility. Indeed, gale-force storms, though more frequent through October to December, are not uncommon from autumn through to spring, while snow can occur at any time of the year. Winter begins in earnest in January and can maintain its hold until May.

However, periods of settled fine weather do visit Skye. In fact, the climate, greatly influenced by the North Atlantic Drift, is generally milder than the Highlands. The weather can be very changeable, which usually provides some variety over the course of a few days.

Mountainous terrain attracts mist and cloud cover, making route-finding difficult – especially where paths are vague or non-existent. High winds and driving rain or snow can blow in with little warning. If there is more than a dusting of snow on the mountains you may need to carry an ice axe and crampons (and know how to use them).

Given that Skye is also known as the Misty Isle for obvious meteorological reasons, the wide range of outstanding walks outwith the island's hillcountry provides plenty of options for when the sun fails to shine.

Access and safety

Public access to the countryside in Scotland is a statutory right. The Scottish Outdoor Access Code provides guidance both for those exercising their right to roam, and for land managers. See the website outdooraccess-scotland.com. Walkers have the right to roam over all open land, but also have responsibilities. Treat the environment and wildlife with care, respect the needs and privacy of those living and working in the country-side, do not obstruct activities such as farming, crofting and deer stalking, and keep dogs under close control near livestock and ground-nesting birds.

In fine weather Skye may seem like paradise; however, the onset of high winds and driving rain, sleet or snow can rapidly make the place feel quite hellish, especially if you are exposed to the elements. Becoming cold and wet rapidly drains body heat, which can lead to hypothermia. It is very important that you are properly equipped and are able to navigate proficiently in poor visibility. Check weather forecasts before setting out and allow yourself plenty of time to complete your walk. Always let someone know your intended route and estimated time of completion.

While a number of the routes featured in this volume keep to clear paths and tracks – some waymarked, others not – there are also those that follow vague and intermittent paths at best, and require a degree of navigational competence. Always take a map and compass or GPS device with you.

Heavy rain and snowmelt can make rivers run very high. Do not attempt to cross rivers in spate. Fast-flowing water which is over knee deep is dangerous. If you're not confident of your ability to get across a river safely, turn around and complete the walk another day. If very wet weather is expected when you plan to head out, you should consider adapting your route and seeking alternatives accordingly.

Getting there and getting around

Skye has been connected to the mainland by the roadbridge between the Kyle of Lochalsh and Kyleakin since 1995. The distance from Glasgow to Portree is around 350km with a journey time of four to five hours, while from Inverness it is approximately 185km and takes around three hours.

Skye can be reached by coach from

Inverness and Fort William with good links to other parts of Scotland. Local bus services operate around many parts of Skye.

There are two car ferry services from the mainland. The Mallaig to Armadale route is operated by Caledonian MacBrayne with up to eight crossings daily in summer, and the small Glenelg to Kylerhea ferry, operated by The Isle of Skye Ferry Community Interest Company, sails from Easter through to mid-October seven days a week.

There is no rail service on Skye. The closest points you can reach by train are Mallaig (for the Armadale ferry) via Glasgow Queen Street and Fort William, or Kyle of Lochalsh via Inverness.

If driving or cycling around Skye, familiarise yourself with the correct use of passing places on the island's single-track roads, including letting vehicles overtake safely.

History

Historical remains, both ancient and more recent, are plentiful on Skye, predominantly scattered around the coastline. Many of the walks in this guidebook visit ancient monuments, including standing stones, chambered cairns, duns, brochs, hut circles and field systems as well as the ruins of more recently abandoned castles, churches and townships.

It is likely that Skye was first occupied during the Mesolithic period – as early as 8000BC – by nomadic hunter-gatherers. The first permanent inhabitants in the Hebrides were the Neolithic people who crossed from continental Europe some 6000 years ago and settled here, raising livestock, clearing woodland and planting crops. Bronze Age and Iron Age peoples followed and around 3000 years ago the first hillforts began appearing on Skye. Defensive settlements provided protection from mainland tribes until they became preoccupied with the Roman presence further south, leading to a more settled period on Skye.

Christianity arrived in the Hebrides with St Columba around 563AD and the early Celtic Christian missionaries set about converting the islands' population. Local Celtic chieftains ruled the islands until the end of the first millennium when the Vikings arrived in the Hebrides. The Norsemen ruled the islands until 1156 when the Norse-Gael warlord, Somerled took control of the Inner Hebrides. The Outer Hebrides remained in Norse hands until they were ceded to the Kingdom of Scotland at the Treaty of Perth in 1266 following the Battle of Largs. Somerled's descendants, Clan MacDonald of Clanranald – known as the Lords of the Isles – emerged as the most important power in northwestern Scotland, ruling their domain as subjects of the King of Scotland. In theory, Clan MacDonald were the feudal superiors of the other Gaelic-speaking clan chiefs who had gradually replaced the Norse princes. However, the power and influence of the clan chiefs was considerable and asserting control over the competing island clans proved difficult.

With the Treaty of Union in 1707, the Hebrides became part of the new Kingdom of Great Britain, although there was significant support for the Stuart cause among the island clan chiefs during the 1715 and 1745 Jacobite rebellions. In 1746 the decisive defeat of Charles Edward Stuart's forces at the Battle of Culloden brought serious repercussions for highlanders and islanders. The British government broke up the clan system and turned the Hebrides into landed estates. The descendants of the clan chiefs became English-speaking landlords more concerned with revenues from their estates than the condition of those living on them. Rents were increased, Gaelic-speaking was discouraged and folk dress was outlawed.

During the 19th century, crofting communities were devastated by the Clearances. Throughout the Highlands and Islands, populations were evicted from the land and replaced with sheep and deer. Large-scale emigration followed, some voluntary, some forced, with islanders relocated to mainland Scotland and the North American colonies. Crop failure and famine in the mid-19th century provoked further emigration. The outlook for the depleted communities remained bleak with excessively high rents, no security of tenure and the denial of land access rights. However, the tide began to turn in the 1870s when crofters and cottars on Lewis and in Wester Ross engaged in 'agitations', including rent strikes and land raids in what became known as the 'land struggles'. Some landless and unemployed islanders were driven to seize land for cultivation in order to survive. Some were arrested and jailed.

By the early 1880s agitation had begun on Skye. In 1882, what started as a demonstration against lack of access to land and eviction notices became a full-scale skirmish between police drafted in from Glasgow and demonstrators, which became known as the Battle of the Braes. This event precipitated the creation of the Napier Commission, which reported in 1884 on the situation of crofters and cottars in the Highlands and Islands. Although the land struggles persisted until after the First World War, the Crofters Act, passed in 1886, forced landowners to make land available for crofting, set fair rents and guaranteed security of tenure and the right to bequeath crofts to a successor.

Nonetheless, emigration continued apace through the 20th century due to unemployment and economic hardship. For those who remained, the economic situation gradually improved and the population decline affecting the Hebrides since the mid-19th century has to some extent stalled in recent years. However, many young people still leave the islands for further education or employment and most don't return. This in turn has resulted in an ageing population.

Today the island economy is largely dependent on the public sector – with a third of all jobs in healthcare, education and services. Local government accounts for another third of the workforce. Farming, crofting, aquaculture, fishing and tourism also remain important sectors of the island economy with the development of renewable energy – wind and wave power projects – a key element of the future island economy.

Natural history

The present-day landscapes of Skye are the product of two major geologic and surface processes. Large-scale tectonic movements during the Paleogene or Lower Tertiary period stretched and thinned the Earth's crust along the western margin of Scotland, precipitating a period of intense volcanic activity some 50 million years ago. Volcanoes formed where magma rose up through fractures in the thinned crust and the resulting extensive lava flows can be seen around Skye today.

During the Pleistocene period, around two million years ago, ice sheets flowed across the landscape, covering most of Britain. On Skye, the glaciers flowed westwards over most of the island and northwards along the east coast, scouring the rocky terrain beneath. Sea levels dropped as fresh waters were locked-up in the advancing ice sheets. The glaciers finally retreated 11,500 years ago and over time the condition of the post-glacial landscape improved as tundra conditions gave way to woodland and mixed vegetation.

Northern Skye, including the Trotternish, Waternish and Duirinish peninsulas, has a plateau-like topography intersected by the sea lochs of Snizort, Dunvegan and Bracadale. Here, Jurassic sedimentary rocks occur, capped by lavas and pyroclastic rocks from the Lower Tertiary period, which dip westwards at a shallow angle. These dip slopes rise to steep scarp slopes at the eastern side, where distinct layers of lava are clearly visible in the exposed rock. Other outstanding features of these rocks are the pinnacles and other landforms in the lee of the Trotternish Ridge, resulting from the landslips that occurred during the Quaternary period, most spectacularly exemplified by the Storr Sanctuary and the Quiraing, which is the largest mass movement slide in Britain, extending over 2km.

However, Skye's most dramatic scenery was created by basalt and gabbro intrusions during the Early Tertiary period that form the jagged topography of the Black Cuillin mountains, which contrast so markedly with the rounded granite forms of the Red Hills on the opposite side of Glen Sligachan. Sleat, the southernmost part of the island, is composed of Lewisian gneiss, Torridonian sedimentary rocks, Moine schists and Cambro-Ordovician sedimentary rocks.

Wildlife

The range of native mammal species present in Skye is broadly the same as in the Highlands. There is a sizeable red deer population, with fallow and roe deer also present. Otters are relatively common with territories around the island's coastline. The rare pine marten has been present in the south and east of the island since the Skye Bridge opened in 1995. Common and Atlantic grey seals are abundant and are often seen basking on offshore rocks and skerries. In the spring and summer months, dolphins and porpoises frequent the sea lochs and minke whales can sometimes be spotted offshore – especially from Rubha Hunish and Waternish Point in the north.

Many birds of prey can be seen, including golden eagle, white-tailed eagle, buzzard, hen harrier, kestrel, merlin, barn owl and short-eared owl.

The other birdlife in Skye is rich, diverse and often spectacular, including a number of rare and uncommon species, native and migrant, such as the corncrake, red-necked phalarope, ptarmigan, red-throated and black-throated divers and the great skua. Seabirds are plentiful and include several of the most impressive and photogenic species, such as gannets and puffins. See www.skye-birds.com for up to date information on recent sightings.

Not all the 'wildlife' is benign; the hugely irritating midge occurs between spring and autumn and is prevalent on windless days. Deer ticks and clegs – an aggressive horsefly with a nasty bite – are the island's other bloodthirsty beasties. Ticks can carry Lyme disease, which can become seriously debilitating if undiagnosed and left untreated. Adders are present, though they are unlikely to bother you unless you bother them first. Be aware, however, as a bite can cause dizziness, vomiting, painful swelling and immobility of an affected limb.

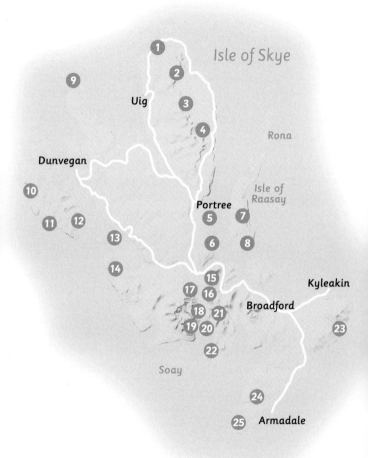

Isle of Skye

Uig

Dunvegan

Portree

Kyleakin

Broadford

Rona

Isle of
Raasay

Soay

Armadale

Contents

Skye

Rubha Hunish

Rubha Hunish

Distance 8.25km **Total ascent** 380m
Time 4 hours **Terrain** moorland,
clifftops and rugged coastline
Map OS Explorer 408 or Harvey
Superwalker Skye: Trotternish
Access bus to Shulista from Portree
(can be caught at Duntulm for the
return). Parking area just off the A855
at the Shulista turning

**Shaped like a stray apostrophe at
the tip of the Trotternish peninsula,
Rubha Hunish is the Isle of Skye's
northernmost point, reaching out
northwestwards towards the Isles
of Lewis and Harris.**

  This rugged, low-lying headland is
hidden away beneath a sheer wall of
towering basalt cliffs rising to its
landward side, revealing itself only once
you reach the overlooking high point of
Meall Tuath. Atop this same vantage
point stands The Lookout, once a
coastguard watch station with
commanding views over The Minch and
now one of the most remarkably
situated of all the Mountain Bothies
Association's (MBA) bothies.

15

The walk out to The Lookout with its tremendous views and the return via the abandoned crofting settlement of Erisco and the ruins of Duntulm Castle makes for a great short excursion, but it is visiting Rubha Hunish itself that really makes this a walk to remember. However, the descent from the clifftops requires some scrambling down a steeply-pitched rocky staircase with some exposure. Happily, this is not as difficult as it looks from above; nonetheless, it is not a descent for the vertiginous. It should also be avoided in wet or icy conditions. The ascent is easier. Sheep and cattle are grazed in the environs so dogs should remain on a lead at all times.

From the parking area just off the A855 at the turning for Shulista, continue over the cattle grid, then immediately turn left on the path signposted for Rubha Hunish. The distinct and well-trodden path is metalled with stone slabs in places and is also waymarked with occasional white-topped posts. Pass a sheep fank and follow the path along the edge of a low heather-clad escarpment, bearing NNW. The path continues along the escarpment, soon crossing a high point overlooking the abandoned village of Erisco below to the left with the prominent ruins of Duntulm Castle atop the rugged promontory of Ru Meanish in Tulm Bay. Go through a metal kissing gate in a stock fence, bear right, then after 400m go through another kissing gate as the path heads into a narrow valley, leading towards the gap between the twin high points of Meall Deas and Meall Tuath. Stay with the main path for another 450m, then turn right on a rough path leading up towards the top of Meall Tuath.

The roof of The Lookout bothy soon comes into view; walk past the fenced-off head of a sheer-sided gully in the cliffs, with splendid views over the Rubha Hunish headland below. Pass a bench on the clifftop on your way to the bothy, which is perched atop the summit of Meall Tuath (116m). The views from here are even better with the prominent sea stack at the edge of Port Lag a' Bhleodhainn the most obvious

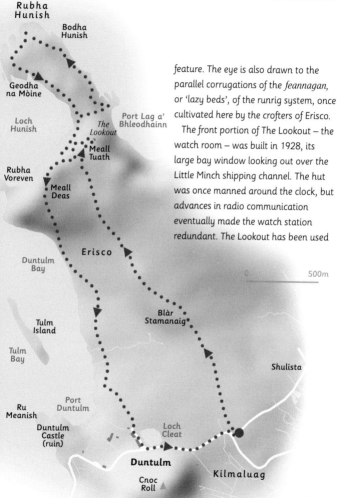

feature. The eye is also drawn to the parallel corrugations of the *feannagan*, or 'lazy beds', of the runrig system, once cultivated here by the crofters of Erisco.

The front portion of The Lookout – the watch room – was built in 1928, its large bay window looking out over the Little Minch shipping channel. The hut was once manned around the clock, but advances in radio communication eventually made the watch station redundant. The Lookout has been used

0   500m

as a bothy since the mid-1970s; when the windows were blown out in a storm in 2005, the MBA stepped in to renovate the building and it has been maintained by volunteers ever since. The bothy sleeps three people on a sleeping platform and bunk-bed arrangement – it has no stove nor hearth and there is no nearby water supply. Always follow the Bothy Code when visiting.

The Lookout's location is spectacular, sitting just a short way back from sheer cliffs that drop 100m straight down to the headland below. There are magnificent views across the water to Gairloch and Wester Ross in the east and the whale-backed hills of Harris and Lewis in the northwest. The bothy is equipped with a chart of whales and other marine mammals that may be spotted in the seas around Rubha Hunish, including dolphins, minke whales, basking sharks and orcas. It is also worth having a wander along the clifftops to the southeast of the bothy for the views of the cliffs and Rubha Hunish itself.

From the bothy, pass by the bench again and follow paths through the heather near the cliff edges – with care – for more tremendous views. Continue down into the gap between Meall Tuath and Meall Deas on an often wet, rocky path. Cross the fence straight ahead on a step stile. If you are not going to descend to the headland then cross a second stile to continue up to the top of Meall Deas. To explore the headland, bear right to go through a metal stock gate near the cliff edge. The steep rocky descent to Rubha Hunish starts here. The first section resembles a rocky staircase and presents a fairly challenging prospect from above, although it's much less alarming once you're actually on it. Keep three-point contact as you scramble carefully down; the route soon bears right, then care is needed as you seek footholds down off the rocks onto the clear path running beneath the cliffs. The path delivers you to the foot of the cliffs, which is littered with broken basalt columns.

Cross the neck of the grassy headland, making for the east coast. The rocky shore platform at the northern end of the shingle beach here features a spectacular igneous dike, a fine geo (or narrow rocky inlet) and a pair of impressive sea stacks. Continue above the cliffs, following the coastline northwestwards for further fine views. The cliffs are home to innumerable seabirds and in the summer months the tip of the headland is a great place for spotting dolphins, porpoise and whales. It's worth circumambulating the entire headland before returning up the path and making the rocky scramble to the clifftops.

Go back through the clifftop gate. If you wish to simply rejoin the outward path, head back to the fence, cross the step stile on the left and bear right to continue through the gap between Meall Deas and Meall Tuath. To complete the full loop, go immediately right through another gate after the clifftop gate to continue uphill, following a path to the top of Meall Deas (100m) with fine views back over Rubha Hunish. The path carries on around the clifftop, then

down to a gateway in a fence corner at the northern edge of Duntulm Bay. Carry on following the vague and often wet path parallel to the foreshore, in the lee of Tulm Island with Duntulm Castle on its rocky headland drawing ever closer. This stretch of coastline is also frequented by seals and otters.

On approaching a drystane dyke, bear left, following a faint path up to its top corner, then turn right and continue past a cattle-feeding bay – this can be churned up – to go through a stock gate. Stay with the wall as you continue until you reach a gateway on your right; go through this, pass a cattle shed and bear left to follow the track past some houses. Carry on through another gate with Loch Cleat on your left and pass a row of white cottages, which are now holiday lets but were formerly occupied by the coastguards who manned The Lookout.

Fork left up to the main road and turn left along this to reach the Shulista turning after 600m.

19

The Needle juts skywards amid
the Quiraing landslips

2

The Quiraing

Distance 6.5km **Total ascent** 465m
Time 3 hours 30 **Terrain** surfaced path
initially, becoming rougher and rockier,
including one easy scramble; the return
along the escarpment is quite exposed
Map OS Explorer 408 or Harvey
Superwalker Skye: Trotternish
Access car park (charge) at the start
on the road from Staffin to Uig

At the northern end of the
Trotternish Ridge lies the otherworldly realm of the Quiraing –
a famously fantastic collection
of geological features arrayed
beneath the steep east-facing
escarpment of Meall na Suiramach.

Its spectacular rock formations were
created after the last glacial period
when the underlying sedimentary rocks
were no longer able to support the
heavier overlying lavas, resulting in a
series of massive landslips. The walk
described here makes the best of this
wonderfully rugged, rocky corner of
Skye. The first short section of surfaced
path from Bealach Ollasgairte soon
gives way to trodden paths leading up

into the craggy fastness of the Quiraing
itself, passing The Prison, The Needle
and The Table among other features,
before climbing to the escarpment top.
There are truly remarkable views to
enjoy the whole way. On days of poor
visibility this walk would be both largely
pointless and potentially hazardous.

The walk starts from the parking area
at Bealach Ollasgairte, the high point of
the minor road linking Staffin and Uig on
the east and west coasts respectively.
Cross to the north side of the road to
join the surfaced path where a large
wooden marker post indicates 'Cuith-
Raing'. It's often busy with visitors along
this first stretch, but the crowds are soon
left behind. As you progress, the views
open up ahead to the spires and
castellations of the Quiraing, and back
along the wave-like crests of the
Trotternish Ridge to the south.

Though rocky in places the narrow
path is distinct and easy to follow as it
runs across the steep slopes below the
cliffs of Maoladh Mòr, soon passing by
the outlying hillock of Cnoc a' Mhèirlich.
The path crosses an often wet and

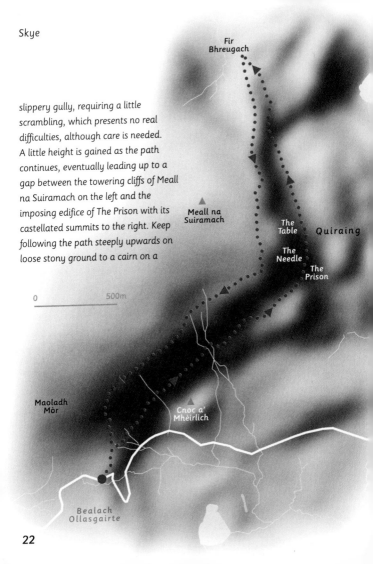

Skye

slippery gully, requiring a little
scrambling, which presents no real
difficulties, although care is needed.
A little height is gained as the path
continues, eventually leading up to a
gap between the towering cliffs of Meall
na Suiramach on the left and the
imposing edifice of The Prison with its
castellated summits to the right. Keep
following the path steeply upwards on
loose stony ground to a cairn on a

Fir
Bhreugach

Meall na
Suiramach

The
Table   Quiraing

The
Needle

The
Prison

0   500m

Maoladh
Mòr

Cnoc a'
Mhèirlich

Bealach
Ollasgairte

narrow bealach at the northern end of The Prison; directly above on the left is the main area of landslips and there is a fine view of the Quiraing's next geological wonder, the rocky pinnacle known as The Needle.

Out of view above The Needle is the third of the Quiraing's most remarkable features, The Table – an expanse of level close-cropped turf sitting atop a raised rock platform, which can also be reached from the main path, although this involves a steep ascent and descent across loose terrain. Such a detour is for the curious and sure-footed only as the return leg of the main route along the escarpment top provides fabulous views down onto The Table and the surrounding crags, stacks and pinnacles.

To reach The Table, head up the steep slope and keep directly left of The Needle. Continue up a broad gully, staying left of a rocky buttress to gain easier ground. The Table lies atop the rocky edifice ahead; it can be reached by passing to the left and following a path up behind its back. Return to the main route by retracing your steps.

Otherwise continue on the main path across the slope, crossing a fence via a stile and soon passing beneath an overhang. The path swings north and continues below further rock formations and pinnacles, although no longer on the same dramatic scale. Pass by a reed-filled lochan, then at a cairn-marked fork in the path where the right branch descends past Loch Hasco and onwards to Flodigarry, keep left and climb a little over a narrow saddle, passing through an old drystane dyke. Continuing through the narrow glen ahead, the path becomes eroded as it climbs steeply up to gain the ridge on the left, crossing a fence on a step stile at the top. If you have the time and energy it's well worth making a detour north along the ridge to visit the prow of Sròn Vourlinn. Otherwise continue south (left), heading up along the edge of the escarpment, keeping safely back from the cliff edge. As you carry on up the stiff, steady gradient, the views over northern Skye just keep improving.

The path is very eroded in places and can be boggy after wet weather. The last section of the climb features a series of rough stone steps. Continuing along the escarpment, the grass-covered top of The Table eventually comes into view below, surrounded by a phalanx of crags, pinnacles and buttresses. Continue following the escarpment edge up to the highest point of the cliffs, which is marked by a large cairn. There are tremendous views of the geological chaos of the Quiraing below and east across the sound to the mountains and coastline of the mainland. For those who wish to visit, the trig point-furnished summit of Meall na Suiramach (543m) lies 300m or so to the west across the moorland plateau.

Keep following the escarpment-top path, which soon descends across an often wet grassy slope to a gate in a fence. Go through and follow the path down across the sloping flank of Maoladh Mòr on a distinct path crossed by a number of stone drainage channels. The descent soon steepens and the path becomes very eroded and boggy in places, requiring care. The rough path eventually meets the good outward path near the start of the walk; turn right to return to Bealach Ollasgairte.

If you have the time, energy and good visibility, you might consider following the path along the escarpment edge climbing away from the south side of the bealach to the summit of Bioda Buidhe (466m) – a round trip of one hour. The views back to the Quiraing are quite fantastic – looking like something out of a Roger Dean poster, if you're of a certain age.

Looking down on the Quiraing from Meall na Suiramach

Looking north along the eastern
escarpment from Bealach Hartaval

3

The Trotternish Ridge

Distance 28.5km **Total ascent** 1900m
Time 10 hours **Terrain** grass and
heather paths most of the way with
some heathery and rocky terrain
Map OS Explorer 408 or Harvey
Superwalker Skye: Trotternish
Access buses to Loch Leathan parking
area from Portree. Return by bus from
the Flodigarry road end, 750m north
of the finish along the A855

Trotternish is Skye's northernmost
peninsula, its coastal strip ringed
with townships, clachans and farms
linked by a single-track road. The
hinterland rises up from the west in
a series of whale-backed spurs to
the mountainous ridge running the
length of the peninsula, then drops
suddenly away over a steep
escarpment of craggy cliffs on the
eastern side to a magical realm of
rock stacks, pinnacles and lochans.

The Trotternish Ridge traverse is one of
the finest ridge walks in the British Isles
yet few walkers are encountered either

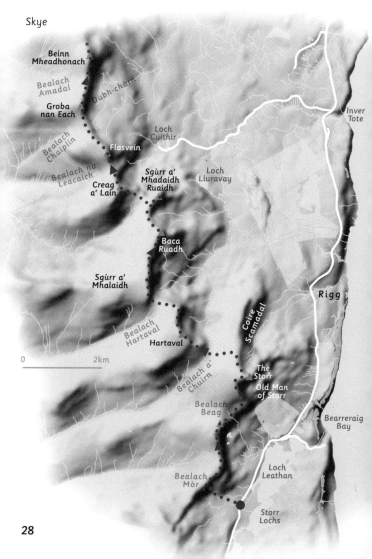

Skye

Beinn Mheadhonach

Bealach Amadal

Dubh-chàrn

Groba nan Each

Bealach Chaiplin

Bealach na Leacaich

Flasvein

Loch Cuithir

Creag a' Lain

Sgùrr a' Mhadaidh Ruaidh

Loch Liuravay

Baca Ruadh

Inver Tote

Sgùrr a' Mhalaidh

0   2km

Bealach Hartaval

Hartaval

Coire Scamadal

Rigg

Bealach a' Chùirn

The Storr
Old Man of Storr

Bealach Beag

Bearreraig Bay

Bealach Mòr

Loch Leathan

Storr Lochs

side of the Storr Sanctuary and the Quiraing, the tourist magnets that bookend the steep eastern escarpment. Though it lacks the fearsome reputation, the technical difficulties and the challenges of the infamous Black Cuillin traverse, the Trotternish Ridge traverse makes for an exhilarating hillwalking experience through a magnificent mountain landscape with some of the finest views in Scotland.

This route joins the ridge just south of The Storr and finishes a few kilometres beyond the Quiraing at Flodigarry, making for a fantastic though demanding day on the hills. The route can be shortened by 4.5km by arranging transport or hitch-hiking from the road crossing the Bealach Ollasgairte. A traverse of the entire ridge from Portree to Uig is also possible, but this 47km route is a tough two-day affair requiring a bivouac along the ridge. Walking the ridge from south to north keeps the prevailing south-westerly winds behind you. It is possible to get off the Trotternish Ridge at various points if necessary; this is

generally safer and easier to the west.

From the small roadside parking area (NG495510) by Loch Leathan, go through a metal stock gate with the Bride's Veil Falls just ahead and follow a path northwest, although this fades as you head across open moorland. Aim to the right of the bealach – the low point on the escarpment top ahead – and as you begin to climb more steeply, make for a path climbing diagonally right to left across the escarpment and follow this up to the ridge, passing through a gate in a stock fence before reaching Bealach Mòr. Now head northeast along the edge of the escarpment, gaining height until you're above the Lochan a' Bhealaich Bhig, nestling at the foot of the cliffs below. Drop a short way into the Bealach Beag, skirting above the bowl scooped out of the escarpment's edge. Begin the steep 260m pull northeastwards up The Storr's grassy southern flank. Near the summit, move closer to the cliff edge for views into Coire Faoin and the Storr Sanctuary with a grandstand view of the Old Man of Storr – a jutting 50m rock pinnacle.

29

Continue to the summit trig point of The Storr, the highest peak of the Trotternish Ridge at 719m. There are fine views east across the sound to the Isles of Rona and Raasay and, on a clear day, the innumerable summits of the mountainous west coast of Scotland.

From the summit, head north-westwards away from the north ridge and descend steadily on good ground towards Bealach a' Chuirn (489m); the view north along the cliffs of the eastern escarpment is particularly dramatic from here. Climb northwestwards from the bealach, steeply at first, then more steadily on grassy slopes to the summit of Hartaval at 669m. The prow-like north ridge of The Storr is impressive from this vantage point. From Hartaval the ridge bends initially northwards, then around to the northwest as you descend to Bealach Hartaval. The next hill on the traverse is Baca Ruadh (639m) with the lower top of Sgùrr a' Mhalaidh (615m) crossed just before the main summit. The promontory of Sgùrr a' Mhadaidh Ruaidh juts northeastwards from the ridge and is reached by following the edge of the escarpment around in a big curve, first northwest, then northeast. The summit (593m) gives fine views along the escarpment, particularly northwards to the distant Quiraing.

Return along the promontory, swinging northwest to continue along the ridge, then descend to a bealach before making the short steep climb to Creag a' Lain (609m). There follows a short descent to Bealach na Leacaich, which is crossed by a fence and dilapidated drystane dyke, before climbing to the whale-backed summit of Flasvein (599m). Drop down into Bealach Chaiplin, then make the short ascent of Groba nan Each (575m). From the summit, continue along the narrowing ridge close to the escarpment edge, avoiding crags on the north-western flank, and descend to Bealach Amadal. Cross Beinn Mheadhonach (579m) to reach Bealach a' Mhòramhain beneath Beinn Edra, the second highest peak on the Trotternish Ridge. The easy ascent along the ridge benefits from a path leading to the summit (611m), where you'll find an

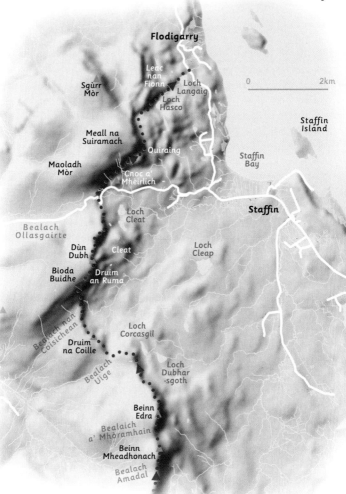

Flodigarry

Leac nan Fionn

Loch Langaig

Sgùrr Mòr

Loch Hasco

0   2km

Meall na Suiramach

Quiraing

Staffin Island

Maoladh Mòr

Cnoc a' Mhèirlich

Staffin Bay

Staffin

Bealach Ollasgairte

Loch Cleat

Loch Cleap

Dùn Dubh

Cleat

Bioda Buidhe

Druim an Ruma

Bealach nan Coisichean

Loch Corcasgil

Druim na Coille

Bealach Uige

Loch Dubhar -sgoth

Beinn Edra

Bealaich a' Mhòramhain

Beinn Mheadhonach

Bealach Amadal

OS trig pillar with a low drystane shelter wall. You can enjoy the view back along the ridge as far as The Storr, then look northwards to Bioda Buidhe and the Quiraing – the final way stations on the day's pilgrimage.

The path continues northwards, keeping close to the cliffs as you descend for over 300m to Bealach Uige – arguably the best camping spot along the ridge. There are small areas of springy grass near the escarpment edge and fresh water can be collected from a small cascade (NG444639) nearby. Continue northwestwards over the slight rise of Druim na Coille at 321m and follow the ridge as it dips down to Bealach nan Coisichean at the foot of Bioda Buidhe's steep southern flank. Climb steeply north with the edge of the escarpment to your right, then as the gradient slackens bear northeast towards the summit of Bioda Buidhe (466m).

From the summit follow a trodden path descending along the escarpment edge. The path follows a cliff edge northwest a short way as it angles obliquely away from the main escarpment. Descend right from this low cliff to follow the main path, which soon continues along the escarpment edge once more – this leads down to a car park on Bealach Ollasgairte (the only road crossing the Trotternish Ridge runs between Uig in the west and Staffin in the east). From the car park cross the road and join a signposted path heading initially northeastwards towards the Quiraing, a Tolkienesque domain of rock stacks and pinnacles. After 1.5km the path leads between a cluster of pinnacles, including the remarkable spire-like Needle above to the left and the sinister edifice of the Prison on the right, which looks very much like Castle Doom on misty days. The path crosses a stile and rounds a bend at an overhanging rock, then continues north through the landslip terrain. A fork in the path is eventually reached, marked with a stone pile cairn; turn right and soon descend past Loch Hasco. Continue on past Loch Langaig before reaching the A855 just south of Flodigarry.

Looking north to the
Quiraing from Bioda Buidhe

Needle Rock (left) and the
Old Man of Storr (centre)

4

The Storr

Distance 8km **Total ascent** 600m
Time 4 hours **Terrain** good paths; some
steep rocky ground in upper reaches;
some danger of rockfalls from the cliffs
above the Old Man; boggy, pathless
moorland on the return
Map OS Explorer 408 or Harvey
Superwalker Skye: Trotternish
Access buses to The Storr parking area
(charge, toilets) from Portree

Rising to 719m, its distinctive form
visible from afar, the summit of The
Storr is the highest point of the
Trotternish Ridge. Beneath the
imposing craggy cliffs of its eastern
flank is an outlandish landscape of
pinnacles and other rock features
known as the Storr Sanctuary.

The steep walk up to the Storr
Sanctuary from the A855 is very
popular with visitors keen for a close
encounter with the huge basalt pinnacle
of the Old Man of Storr, one of Skye's
best-known and most-photographed
landscape features, which stands 50m
from base to summit.

In fact, the Old Man – or Bodach an

Stoir – is the most prominent of an array of striking rock features in the Sanctuary, including Needle Rock, which were left standing in the aftermath of ancient landslips. Indeed, the Trotternish Ridge is the longest geological landslip in Britain. The area is composed mainly of ancient lava flows, which can be seen in the horizontal layering on The Storr's exposed cliff faces. The landslips were caused by the underlying sedimentary rocks collapsing under the weight of the dense volcanic basalt, tipping the layers sideways.

The route described here visits some of the best viewpoints in the Storr Sanctuary. As well as the remarkable landscape of the Sanctuary itself, there are also tremendous views out over the Sound of Raasay to the Isle of Raasay and the mainland beyond. Of the many people visiting the Sanctuary, few continue on the climb to The Storr's imposing summit — for those with the time and energy, leaving the crowds behind and enjoying the superlative views from the 719m summit is highly recommended.

From The Storr car park on the A855 between Portree and Staffin, go through a gate to join the broad gravelled path, which winds its way uphill through cleared forestry. Keep right at a fork and climb along the sinuous path, eventually passing through a gate; as you gain height, there are grand views eastwards back to the Isles of Raasay and Rona with Applecross on the mainland beyond. The path eventually zigzags its way up the steep slopes to a gate in a deer fence; go through and continue across the open moorland with the spectacular craggy cliffs of The Storr rising ahead.

Carry on up the broad path; at this point the Old Man can be difficult to pick out against the backdrop of cliffs. As the path rises, look out for a distinct path forking left and leave the main route here. The path contours a little before a steepening climb and eventually arrives at a small col close to the Old Man with the main cliffs of The Storr directly above. Climb up to the left of the Old Man, but not directly up to its base, keeping left at a fork. From

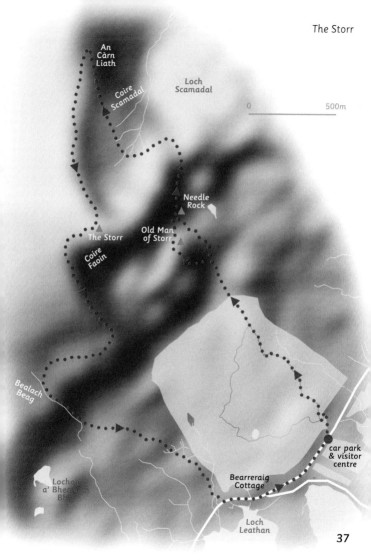

An Càrn
Liath

Coire
Scamadal

Loch
Scamadal

0   500m

Needle
Rock

The Storr

Old Man
of Storr

Coire
Faoin

Bealach
Beag

car park
& visitor
centre

Bearreraig
Cottage

Lochan
a' Bhenchan
Bheag

Loch
Leathan

this vantage point the towering pinnacle is immensely impressive, resembling a huge leaning menhir with its tapering top. Undercut by erosion at its base, the Old Man appears to be on the verge of toppling. It was first climbed in 1955 by the renowned mountaineer, Don Whillans, by a route that is still classified as Very Severe.

As there is some risk from rockfall along the next part of the route, it should be approached with caution (and indeed avoided after heavy rain or freezing conditions). After descending into a dip as it passes behind the Old Man, the path is distinct but briefly crosses a short stretch of fallen rocks. This area, amid towering cliffs and rock pinnacles, is known as the Storr Sanctuary. Ahead stands the rather Gothic-looking Needle Rock, also known as 'the Cathedral' – a gravity-defying, castellated slab of rock, which has a pair of 'windows' right through it near the top. Pass behind Needle Rock and continue along the path leading north, staying below the cliffs, to reach a small col where a stile crosses a fence. Head

over to the knoll on the right for the view back to the Old Man and Needle Rock with the Storr Lochs beyond.

If you don't want to continue to The Storr, return from the knoll to the col and then head back down the path behind Needle Rock to rejoin the main path and continue back to the car park.

To continue to The Storr, from the stile follow the path round to the left, then fork left to climb over a band of rocky terrain. Once above this rocky obstacle the going is much easier as the path contours around the amphitheatre of Coire Scamadal. After around 1km, a small cairn marks a sharp left-hand turn up across grassy slopes to gain The Storr's broad north ridge. Once on the ridge, climb steadily southwards to reach the summit, marked by an OS trig point.

The views are glorious – the Trotternish Ridge winds its sinuous course northwards with the Harris Hills sometimes visible beyond; to the east lie the islands of Raasay and Rona, with a phalanx of mainland summits as a backdrop, while to the south the contrasting rough and smooth profiles of the Black and Red Cuillin mountains are prominent.

From the summit, continue initially southwestwards above the towering cliffs. Pass around the head of a wide, steep scree gully before turning south-eastwards to descend steadily along the escarpment edge with excellent views over the Storr Sanctuary and the Old Man below. Stay with the escarpment edge as it turns southwestwards once again, reaching a gully where a burn drops down the cliffs after around

500m. A distinct path descends along the nearside of the burn – it is steep and very rough, but presents no difficulties.

Follow the path down beneath the escarpment cliffs, then continue descending southeastwards across the moorland, following paths where possible, with cleared forestry ahead to the left. Make for a gate leading into a small gravelled parking area next to the A855 road. On reaching the road, turn left and follow the roadside path northwards for 500m to arrive back at The Storr car park.

The spires and pinnacles of the Storr Sanctuary
beneath the sheer cliffs of The Storr

Ben Tianavaig

Distance 7km **Total ascent** 530m
Time 3 hours 30 **Terrain** unmarked
trodden paths and sheep tracks; care
is needed on exposed cliff edges,
especially in windy conditions
Map OS Explorer 410 **Access** bus to
Braes from Portree; get off at the
Camustianavaig road end, 1km from the
start **Note** steep cliffs and grazing sheep
mean dogs are not allowed on the hill

**Standing sentinel over the Sound
of Raasay, the elegantly sculpted
summit of Ben Tianavaig rises
from the sea in oblique layers of
volcanic rock.**

It is an outstanding hill in every sense,
given its outlying position and the
literally breathtaking views that this
affords. Surprisingly, however, this is
a hill that attracts many more
superlatives than actual visitors. Given
the hill's modest height, the relative
brevity of the route and ease of access,
it's a wonder that it isn't more popular.

Lying just to the south of Portree
and Loch Portree, Ben Tianavaig is,
geologically and geographically

Ben Tianavaig

43

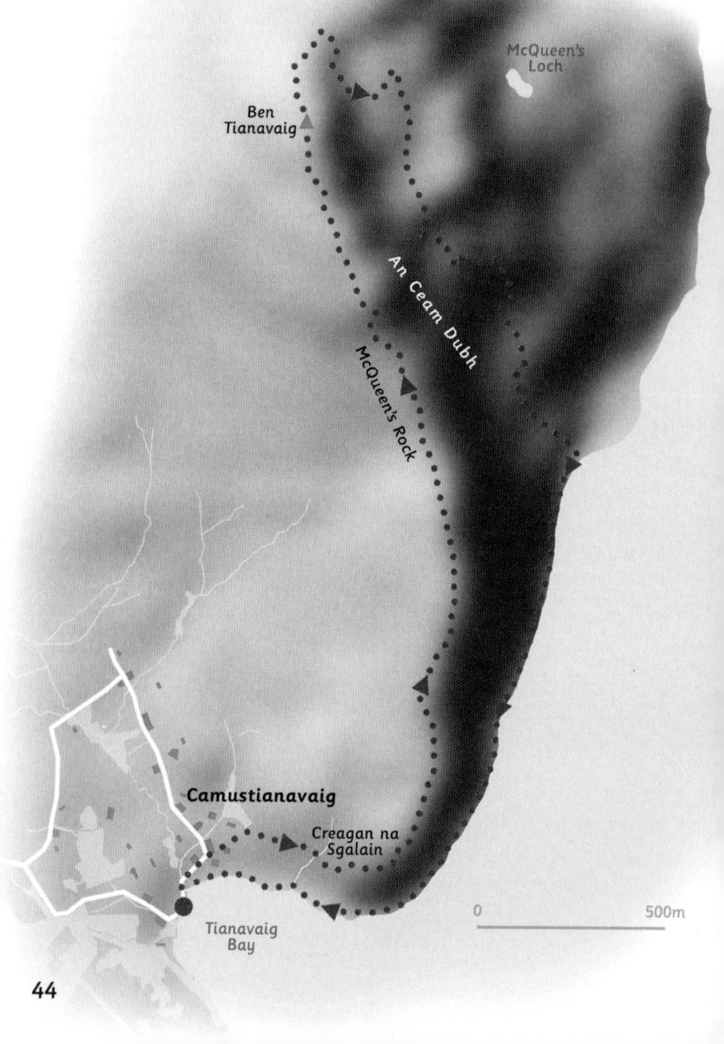

Skye

McQueen's
Loch

Ben
Tianavaig

An Ceam Dubh

McQueen's Rock

Camustianavaig

Creagan na
Sgalain

Tianavaig
Bay

0   500m

speaking, the full stop beneath the long exclamation mark of the Trotternish Ridge. The eastern flank of the hill has the same sheer cliffs and characteristic landslips, replete with rock stacks and pinnacles, while its western slopes are heather-clad peat moorland.

Starting from the sheltered coastal settlement of Camustianavaig, this walk climbs out along the airy escarpment edge to the summit of Ben Tianavaig with its commanding views across Skye, Raasay and beyond. Although you can simply retrace your steps from here, a more engaging return descends across the landslips beneath the escarpment and down to the shore before following the coast back to Tianavaig Bay. Apart from a brief exposed section above a steep drop, this return presents no difficulties and though there are no actual paths, sheep tracks aid progress and the going is generally easy underfoot.

From the parking area next to the stony shore, head north a short way to the second bend, then turn right off the road by the red postbox. Turn left in front of a metal gate across a driveway and head up the path (a small sign reads 'Hill Path') through a fenced break between houses and a stand of rowan trees. The path can become a stream in wet weather. Continue to a wooden gate in a boundary fence and follow the path bearing right up the steep heathery slope. Where the incline levels the path forks with both branches leading uphill. Follow the more distinct right-hand branch towards a pronounced rocky hummock ahead, which proves to be on the cliff edge. Now continue climbing northwards along the edge of the steep escarpment, following trodden paths – there are views back over Camustianavaig.

As you carry on along the cliff edge, the rough moorland terrain gives way to close-cropped turf with distinct sheep-tracks easing the steady climb towards the summit. An exposed section requires care above a big drop down to the sea – either keep to the edge of the escarpment with its dramatic views, or follow a slightly easier parallel path to the left. As you progress ever higher, the views open up back towards the Red Hills and the Black Cuillin, while virtually the whole of Raasay is laid out below across the narrow sound.

Follow the cliff edge path along McQueen's Rock, with the summit trig point of Ben Tianavaig soon coming into view. Below the steep slopes to the east is a realm of small pinnacles and curious rocky outcrops – like a small-scale version of the Storr Sanctuary.

On reaching the summit, which is marked by a cylindrical 'Vanessa' trig point, the views expand yet further. Although Ben Tianavaig stands at a modest 413m, the panorama is extraordinary. Portree and its picturesque harbour appears to the northwest, with The Storr and its rocky amphitheatre beyond, but it is the view back along the escarpment and across the sound to the Red Hills and the Black Cuillin that takes all the prizes.

The quickest and easiest option for returning to Camustianavaig is to retrace your outward route, or follow the path running parallel to the escarpment edge just to the right.

This option also has the advantage of tremendous views ahead for much of the return.

Alternatively, if you're sure-footed and don't mind a little exposure, the route described here makes a longer less-straightforward but stimulating return down through the rocky outcrops beneath the escarpment. Continue northwards from the summit, descending along the cliffs for around 400m and then down to a bealach at the head of a grassy valley running beneath the escarpment. From here, it is possible to descend the steep slopes of An Ceam Dubh below Ben Tianavaig's cliffs. Keep to the valley's outer edges initially, the better to explore the pinnacles and rock formations and to avoid the rough, bouldery ground in the middle. Eventually sheep tracks lead out of this enchanting amphitheatre, down steep grassy slopes to a prominent green pasture by the shore.

A distinct, narrow sheep-frequented path leads southwards along the coast, soon climbing above the shore. In places it may look as if the way will become impassable, but the path continues unbroken across the slopes. As you round the southern end of the Ben Tianavaig escarpment, the slope becomes very steep beneath the rocky outcrops of Creagan na Sgalain. Where the path climbs to the base of the rocky cliffs there is a narrow exposed section above a sheer drop to the rocky beach below. Continue up above a small stand of birch trees and follow the trodden path, which eventually descends to a gate on the left by the shoreline. Go through and continue round to the stony beach in Tianavaig Bay. The path is overgrown in places, but if you stick with it you will eventually emerge on the beach – either cross the outflow of the burn or head right along the bank to the road by the bridge. If the tide is against you, walk behind the houses to rejoin the outward path.

Ben Tianavaig and The Storr (right)
seen from Churchton Bay, Raasay

Ben Tianavaig

Skye

An Àird, Braes

6

An Àird

Distance 4km **Total ascent** 150m
Time 2 hours **Terrain** good path to the
beach; pathless and boggy in places on
the peninsula **Map** OS Explorer 410
Access bus from Portree to the
Balmeanach turning on the main Braes
road, 1km from the start

The east coast townships of the
Braes look out across the sound to
the neighbouring island of Raasay.
The Narrows of Raasay are just
1km wide at the closest point
between the islands where the
An Àird peninsula juts eastwards
into the strait.

It's worth factoring in plenty of time
for the relatively short walk around this
fascinating peninsula with its fine coastal
scenery, interesting geological features
and exceptional views in all directions.
This is also a great spot for watching
seals and seabirds, while dolphins can
also sometimes be seen in the narrows.

The peninsula is, in fact, a tombolo, a
deposition landform created when a spit
or sandbar gradually extends as
sediments are deposited by longshore

drift, eventually forming an isthmus joining an offshore island. This geomorphological process is apparent in the way the isthmus slopes and tapers towards the tied island of the An Àird peninsula.

Travelling south along the Braes road, take the left-hand turn signposted for Gedintailor, Balmeanach and Peinachorrain. Continue along the minor road past houses for 500m to a long passing place with a red postbox on the left. Park at one end with care so as not to obstruct the passing place or the road. Follow the path heading east from the passing place across rough grassland, which soon descends a steep grassy slope to the shore at Camas a' Mhòr-bheòil, passing a bench on the way.

The path runs out by the shore beneath the grassy ramparts of the isthmus. A pebble beach fringes the bay, with the tip of the An Àird peninsula at its extremity. Continue eastwards around the beach, which reveals a sandy foreshore at low tide. At the far end of the beach keep following the coastline on grassy ground, which can be boggy in places. Pass Loch an Amadain lying to landward, then continue along low broken cliffs towards the tip of the peninsula.

The northern end of An Àird is soon reached, crowned by Dùnan an Aisilidh, the site of an ancient fort of uncertain age, although scattered stones are all that now remain of its walls. From this splendid vantage point, there are views east across the Narrows of Raasay to the Isle of Raasay and north to the tiered slopes of Ben Tianavaig, a geological outlier of the Trotternish Ridge. Seals can often be seen in the narrows here and, less-frequently, dolphins and porpoises.

Once you're done absorbing the views, turn south to continue along the east coast of the peninsula. The cliffs here may be low but they're big on fine coastal scenery with lots of interesting features, especially at the far end of the peninsula. Towards the southern end of An Àird there are a couple of natural arches, caves, stacks and a blowhole. It's worth taking a close look at these features, but exercise caution near the cliff edges. The coastline soon turns westwards, heading towards the southern shore of the isthmus; there are tremendous views of Glamaig and the Red Hills to the south.

Descend towards the beach fringing the southern shore. You can head across the narrow neck of land here to the northern shore to retrace your outward route to the start, but for variety this route returns along the top of the grassy rampart above the shore, following trodden paths. Follow the outside of a stock fence where it turns in right angles above the head of a grassy gully. Where it turns sharply inland definitively, continue northwestwards, following a

trodden path around the head of another gully, which can be a bit boggy. Carry on along the top of the grassy slopes until you rejoin the outward path from Balmeanach which you follow back to the start.

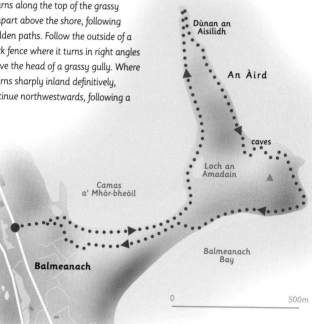

Dùnan an Aisilidh

An Àird

caves

Loch an Amadain

Camas a' Mhòr-bheòil

Balmeanach Bay

Balmeanach

0   500m

Dùn Caan seen from the south

7

Dùn Caan

Distance 23km **Total ascent** 770m
Time 7 hours 30 **Terrain** open moorland,
drovers' tracks and minor roads
Map OS Explorer 409 **Access** regular
ferry to Churchton Bay from Sconser

**It's easy to overlook Skye's next
door neighbour, Raasay (or
Ratharsair in Scottish Gaelic) when
drawn by the siren call of the Cuillin
and Skye's multifarious other
attractions, but a short ferry ride
across the Narrows of Raasay
delivers those with the requisite
curiosity to a smaller island with
a distinctive geography, varied
geology and a character all its own.**

The island is 23km long north to south
and 5km east to west at its widest point
– the distinctive cockscomb summit of
Dùn Caan is Raasay's highest point at
443m. The island of Rona lies just off
Raasay's north coast and the tidal islets
of Eilean Fladday and Eilean Tigh are to
the northwest, while Scalpay lies 1.5km
to the southeast. Raasay House sits in
its grounds at Clachan, overlooking
Churchton Bay and the ferry pier. The

island has a population of around 190
and the main settlement is at Inverarish.

The shorter 'out-and-return' route to
Dùn Caan (5 hours) has clear paths for
most of the way and is not especially
demanding. This 23km circular route via
Hallaig requires a degree of navigational
competence as there are pathless
sections. Either option takes in
magnificent scenery – not least the
views west to Skye's Red Cuillin and
the Trotternish Ridge. The longer route,
which loops around the southern part
of Raasay, is rather modest to start
with, following minor roads and
moorland paths. Once you reach the
summit of Dùn Caan, however, the walk
takes on an air of grandeur with
dramatic landscapes, glorious views
and the poignant vestiges of the
abandoned settlement at Hallaig.
Between 5.5km and 6km of road-
walking can be saved on the return leg
if you can arrange transport from North
Fearns or Eyre respectively.

CalMac operate the ferry between
Sconser on Skye and Churchton Bay
pier on Raasay. The crossing takes 15

minutes and ferries are fairly frequent in summer. If walking the longer route, take an early ferry to give yourself plenty of time – unless you are staying on Raasay.

From the pier, bear right past the toilets and continue along Pier Road, ignoring left and right turnings. At a T-junction in front of a large quadrangular 19th-century steading with an Italianate clocktower, bear right (signposted Inverarish) and follow the lane past the Isle of Raasay Distillery buildings – hopefully you'll have time to visit on your return. Continue to a fork by some houses and turn left along the Hallaig Road. Follow the road, passing more houses, then bear right at a fork by an information panel. Continue over an old stone bridge, then keep straight on (left) at a fork signposted Fearns – with The North Pole indicated back the way you've walked from. Keep straight ahead along the road, which soon climbs past the concrete piers of a derelict viaduct – part of the incline railway that served the island's long-defunct ironstone mine, which was

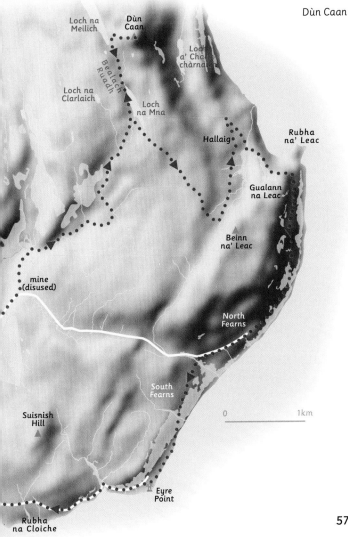

Loch na
Meilich

Dùn
Caan

Loch
a' Chadha
chàrnach

Bealach
Ruadh

Loch na
Clarlaich

Loch
na Mna

Hallaig

Rubha
na' Leac

Gualann
na Leac

Beinn
na' Leac

mine
(disused)

North
Fearns

South
Fearns

Suisnish
Hill

0   1km

Eyre
Point

Rubha
na Cloiche

worked by German POWs during the First World War. You reach the top of the road after 1km by the derelict buildings of No1 mine; turn left through a gateway and over a cattle grid, following Burma Road – so-called by the forestry workers who built the road through woodland here in the 1950s. Go straight ahead, crossing a bridge, ignore turns to left and right, cross another bridge, then at a path junction turn right (signposted Dùn Cana) and climb alongside the Inverarish Burn.

Go through a gate and follow the path across open moorland. The gradient is fairly gentle and the generally distinct path mostly stays close to the burn – it can be a bit boggy in its upper reaches. The path eventually crosses a fence via a stile, soon reaching Loch na Mna with the cockscomb ridge of Dùn Caan beyond. Ignore the path climbing onto the escarpment above the loch; instead follow a path above the shore to the head of the loch where an area of boulders needs to be crossed with care. Beyond the boulders a vague, often boggy path leads across Bealach Ruadh

beneath the escarpment to Loch na Meilich; continue on the path heading diagonally uphill to the right of the loch. The path doubles back to the right, then zigzags up the steep western flank of Dùn Caan to its rocky summit (443m), which is marked by a cylindrical 'Vanessa' triangulation pillar. In clear conditions the views are magnificent, especially southwest to the Red Cuillin and northwest to Ben Tianavaig and the Trotternish Ridge. Retrace your outward route if you wish to return to the pier.

To continue to Hallaig, return past Loch na Mna, then leave the path through a metal gate. Head southeast with care across boggy moorland and pick up a vague path along the upper edge of the landslips tumbling down towards Hallaig and the east coast. Follow the intermittently boggy path along to the bealach below Beinn na' Leac and then descend northwards to the left of the Hallaig Burn. Keep left of the woodland towards the bottom of the gorge. Here, you will find the ruins of the abandoned settlement of Hallaig. There are fine views of the steep cliffs rising above Raasay's eastern shores.

From the bottom easternmost corner of the vast drystane-walled enclosure, follow a trodden path southeast down to cross the Hallaig Burn and then take a path southwards up through a birchwood. Cross a clearing and follow the path into gnarly, lichen-draped birch woodland, passing the ruin of a fine stone-built stable. The path continues beneath impressive limestone cliffs and soon comes to a memorial cairn commemorating the Raasay-born poet, Sorley MacLean, and his poem 'Hallaig'. Continue along the old grassy drovers' track, which swings south and then southwest, until it reaches the road at North Fearns. The views ahead across the sound to the Red Hills are tremendous. Stay with the road for 800m, then turn left onto an unmarked path just beyond the last white-painted house. Cross the burn and contour along the hillside above woodlands for 800m before descending obliquely through the woods to pick up a path just above the shore. Continue along the coast towards the lighthouse beacon at Eyre Point.

Just before reaching the beacon, bear right along a grassy path, then left along a track. Go through a gate to join the road. Follow the road for 6km back to the Churchton Bay pier, forking left downhill to pass the old pier at East Suisnish and turning left (signposted The North and Clachan) at a junction at Inverarish. The tramp along the road is greatly enlivened by the superb views across to Skye.

Skye

Returning along the Hallaig path at North Fearns with Skye's Red Hills across the sound

Hallaig

Distance 7.5km **Total ascent** 435m
Time 3 hours 30 **Terrain** waymarked
grassy path for much of the way; vague
paths only to the ruins of Hallaig; the
return around Beinn na' Leac is rough
and pathless in places **Map** OS Explorer
409 **Access** ferry to Churchton Bay from
Sconser; parking at North Fearns road
end; no public transport to the start of
the walk – it is a 5.5km walk from
Churchton Bay to North Fearns

**The abandoned village of Hallaig is
tucked into an exceptionally
beautiful fold of Raasay's coastline
beneath a magnificent sweep of
escarpment at the island's
uninhabited southeast corner.**

The wooded Hallaig Burn tumbles
down from the bealach between the heel
of Beinn na' Leac and the long ridge
running up to the crest of Dùn Caan to
the northwest. The poignant ruins of this
long-deserted township look out over the
Inner Sound to the coast and mountains
of Applecross, while the wooded cliffs of
Raasay's east coast stretch away to the
north. This once-thriving settlement was

61

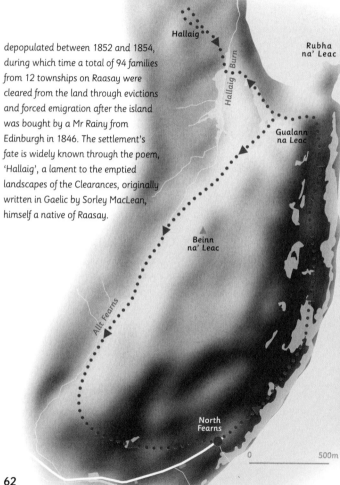

Skye

depopulated between 1852 and 1854, during which time a total of 94 families from 12 townships on Raasay were cleared from the land through evictions and forced emigration after the island was bought by a Mr Rainy from Edinburgh in 1846. The settlement's fate is widely known through the poem, 'Hallaig', a lament to the emptied landscapes of the Clearances, originally written in Gaelic by Sorley MacLean, himself a native of Raasay.

Hallaig

Rubha na' Leac

Hallaig Burn

Gualann na Leac

Beinn na' Leac

Allt Fearns

North Fearns

0   500m

The walk out to Hallaig is most often undertaken as an out-and-back route. The circular alternative described here is more demanding but adds an extra dimension.

By the parking area next to the final house at the road end in North Fearns, a wooden signpost indicates Hallaig. Continue along the well-constructed grass track, which runs high above the shore along the island's east coast, with views to the Crowlin Islands and the mountains of the mainland across the Inner Sound. The gently undulating bracken-fringed path makes for generally easy going underfoot, although it can be wet in places.

After 2km or so, the track swings left beneath an impressive limestone cliff where a cairn commemorates Sorley MacLean with a brass plaque bearing the words of 'Hallaig', his most celebrated poem, in both Gaelic and English. The site of the abandoned township itself lies a further 1km to the northwest on the slopes beneath the crags and cliffs flanking Dùn Caan.

Continue along the path, soon entering birch woodland and passing the ruins of a stone-built stable. Cross a clearing with the corrugations of old lazy beds still apparent and enter a second swathe of birchwood as the well-built track gives way to a rough path. Pass through the woodland and then emerge into another clearing. Where the path forks, keep right and descend through birch trees to cross the Hallaig Burn flowing down through its wooded gully. Once across, follow the faint, often muddy path climbing away from the burn. On emerging from the trees, make for the bottom corner of a huge drystane-dyked enclosure and follow this uphill to reach a stone-built byre. Continue to the right to explore the ruins of Hallaig – the stone walls and grassed-over footings of houses and byres scattered across the grassy terraces.

On a fine day it's hard to imagine a more idyllic site for a settlement, bounded to landward by wooded slopes and cliffs capped by the cockscomb summit of Dùn Caan, with an outlook across the Inner Sound to the mainland mountains and northwards along

Raasay's dramatic east coast. Hallaig was at one time likely the largest township on Raasay. Archaeological surveying records some 80 structures at the site, comprising 44 ruined houses, as well as byres, stores and enclosures. The most outstanding feature is the large post-Clearance stone-built sheep fank, which was built with stones taken from some of the houses after the village was cleared in 1854. There are also large areas of lazy beds on the slopes above the village to the west

You can retrace your outward route to North Fearns, but the return described here makes for a longer, more demanding circular walk – paths are unmarked, often vague and intermittent, so a little navigational competence is required. The going is also rough at times with dense heather cover and rocky ground.

From the site of Hallaig, head initially southwards up the slopes following paths through the heather and bracken as best you can. Then trend SSW, aiming towards the bealach between Beinn na' Leac and the buckled moorland escarpment running up to the crest of Dùn Caan. Once you've reached the bealach, follow the trodden path along a prominent natural dyke running southwestwards along the flank of Beinn na' Leac. Having crossed the bealach, keep your height, contouring around the flank of the hill rather than dropping into the broad gully through which the Allt Fearns flows. Carry on following the rough path southwestwards until you see a gap on the left with a knoll to its right. Cross the southwest flank of Beinn na' Leac here and continue steeply down the hillside, making for the road at North Fearns below.

Dùn Caan rising above the ruins of Hallaig

Looking south along the west coast
of the Waternish peninsula

Waternish Point

Distance 13.5km **Total ascent** 415m
Time 4 hours **Terrain** outward route on
farm track; final section to Waternish
Point crosses largely pathless, grassy
and heathery ground; the return along
the clifftops is generally firm and dry
Map OS Explorer 407 **Access** no public
transport to the start. Parking opposite
the burial ground at Trumpan Church

**On fine days the uninhabited
northernmost part of the Waternish
peninsula has an air of tranquillity
about it. The absence of roads
combined with expansive seascapes
and big skies make for a peaceful
atmosphere, somewhat at odds
with its often brutal history.**

  This not particularly demanding half-
day walk passes the sites of battles, a
massacre and a township abandoned
during the Clearances. A pair of ruined
Iron Age brochs also passed en route
add to the palpable presence of history
on the peninsula. In late summer and
early autumn the dense purple carpet of

flowering heather sets the headland aglow. Waternish Point is also a great spot for cetacean-watching with whales and dolphins regularly spotted in the waters of the Little Minch. The route, which largely follows a farm track and grassy clifftop paths, is generally easy going, though the track and the moorland between Bail' an Tailleir and the lighthouse can be boggy in places after wet weather. Plenty of sheep and cattle are grazed here, so keep dogs on a lead.

The walk starts opposite the forlorn ruin of Trumpan Church, which serves as a monument to one of the bloodiest episodes in Skye's history. Trumpan was once a thriving medieval township and its simple rectangular church, founded in the 1300s, was its focal point until the life of both township and church was snuffed out on the first Sunday in May 1578. While the local MacLeods were gathered for worship in the church, the MacDonalds of Uist were mooring their boats in nearby Ardmore Bay. The previous year 395 MacDonalds were massacred in a cave on the Isle of Eigg by MacLeods. Taking their revenge, the MacDonalds barricaded the doors of the packed church and set the roof thatch ablaze. All the MacLeods within perished, save for a young girl who escaped through a window. She fled to Dunvegan and raised the alarm, whereafter an army of MacLeods set forth for Trumpan, their mystical Fairy Flag unfurled, and massacred the MacDonalds in turn. By way of burial the MacDonald corpses were lined up behind a drystane dyke, which was then toppled over on them – hence the battle became known as 'The Spoiling of the Dyke'.

From the parking area opposite the church, head northeast along the road, passing several houses before reaching a sharp bend after 500m. Turn left along the farm track here and go through a gate. The track is initially well-drained, but can be boggy in places further out into the heather-mantled moorland. Go through an old metal gate and after 1.25km you reach a cairn on a hillock to the left of the track. A plaque commemorates Roderick MacLeod,

Waternish Point

killed during the second Battle of Waternish in 1530. A short distance further along the track, a large stone ruin is visible up on the moor to the right. It is worth making a detour to visit Dùn Borrafiach, an Iron Age broch with its great stone walls still standing more than 3m high.

Return to the track and continue northwards for another 1km or so before passing the ruin of another broch up on a grassy mound on the right. It is considerably more dilapidated than Dùn Borrafiach with only the first course or two of the walls surviving – doubtless much of the stone was plundered over the years for building enclosures, dykes and shielings. Close inspection of the site reveals a hole in the ground with a short section of passageway that still has its roof. As is often the case with the strategic positioning of brochs, Dùn Gearymore provides a wonderful viewpoint, particularly across the Little Minch towards the Outer Isles. Return once again to the track and continue northwards.

A shortcut is soon available if you bear left along a path off the track before it bends right. A narrow grassy path leads towards a gap in a turf dyke. Follow the faint path towards a gap in a drystane dyke; beyond this the firm grassy ground along the clifftop makes for excellent walking. On meeting a fence, follow it until it comes to a gate; go through and continue towards the lighthouse at Waternish Point.

Otherwise stay with the track, which soon swings northeastwards as it continues across the moorland. Pass by some ruined blackhouses and continue through a gap in a drystane dyke – which is often very boggy – to grazing pasture with further ruins of an abandoned settlement. Continue following a grassy path obliquely right across the pasture, crossing a channel, to the austere ruin of Unish House. Once the most significant house in Waternish, it was originally built around 1605 before being renovated in the early 18th century when the size of the windows was increased and a stair tower was added. It was likely built by one of the so-called Fife Adventurers, Lowland noblemen who were encouraged by King James VI to colonise parts of north-west Scotland, which accounts for some stylistic similarities with architecture in Fife. Built without defences or battlements, Unish was said to have been the earliest domestic residence in Skye. The sizeable township that grew up around the big house; Bail 'an Tailleir, or Tailor's Town, included some 47 buildings, although the settlement was relatively short-lived as the area was subjected to the 19th-century

Clearances visited on much of the Highlands and Islands. The house was abandoned and fell into disrepair in the late 19th century; it is now in a very poor state, so care should be taken around the building.

From the ruins of Unish House continue northwestwards across the pasture, go through a stock gate on the right, then soon cross a gap in an old drystane dyke. Now follow paths through the heather-cloaked moorland, which is a riot of purple in late summer and early autumn – although the ground can be boggy in places. Continue all the way to the white-painted automated lighthouse, which is powered by solar panels. Waternish Point is a place of expansive island-dotted seascapes. This is also an excellent site for cetacean-spotting. Minke whales, dolphins and porpoises are frequently seen here, while orca have occasionally been spotted. There are also seabirds aplenty to be seen, including gannets with their impressive dive-bombing displays.

For the return leg of the walk, it is worth staying along the clifftops on the western side of the peninsula for the springy turf underfoot and the superb views south along the coast to Dunvegan Head and west across the Little Minch to Uist. Continue southwards, soon passing through a gate in a stock fence. Follow the paths along the clifftops with care, crossing occasional burns, for around 4km until you reach a deeper gully bearing the Borrafiach Burn, a natural barrier diverting you across the moor towards the memorial cairn passed on the outward route. On regaining the track, retrace your outward route to the start.

Skye

Heading to the lighthouse
on Waternish Point

Waterstein Head dominates
the Duirinish coast

The Hoe and Waterstein Head

Distance 15km **Total ascent** 675m
Time 6 hours 30 **Terrain** pathless
moorland and clifftops; care is needed,
especially in windy conditions
Map OS Explorer 407 **Access** bus
from Portree to the Ramasaig road end,
5.25km from the start

**Between Dunvegan Head in the
north and Idrigill Point in the south,
the magnificent Duirinish coastline
is frequently breathtaking and
seldom less than dramatic.**

Facing westwards across The Little
Minch to the islands of Uist, the mighty
triumvirate of sea cliffs rising between
Neist Point and Lorgill Bay comprise
Waterstein Head, Ramasaig Cliff and
The Hoe. Each of these outstanding
clifftop summits are visited during the
course of this walk, although there are
shorter less demanding options.

The clifftop sections of this route are
very exposed at times and great care is
needed along the cliff edges of The Hoe
and Hoe Rape, which are not protected
by fences – this is not a walk for a very
windy day. On account of the

considerable numbers of sheep and
cattle encountered, occasional barbed-
wire fences to be crossed and the sheer
cliffs, this is not an ideal walk for dogs.

From Glendale, continue southwest
along the B884 signposted for
Waterstein and Neist Point, then take
the minor road on the left signposted
for Ramasaig. The road is rough and
extensively potholed, needing careful
driving, especially if your car has little
clearance. Park tidily near the house at
the end of the public road – there is a
stock gate across the road here. Go
through the kissing gate next to the
stock gate – with a sign for Lorgill –
and continue along the road, passing
an agricultural shed and a sheep fank.
Cross the bridge over the Ramasaig
Burn and continue as tarmac gives way
to unsurfaced track. Pass a stone-built
byre, keeping left along the main track,
and go through a gate. This part of the
track is usually churned up around a
cattle-feeding bay.

Continue for a little over 2km until just
before a gate where the track begins to
descend towards Lorgill. Leave the track

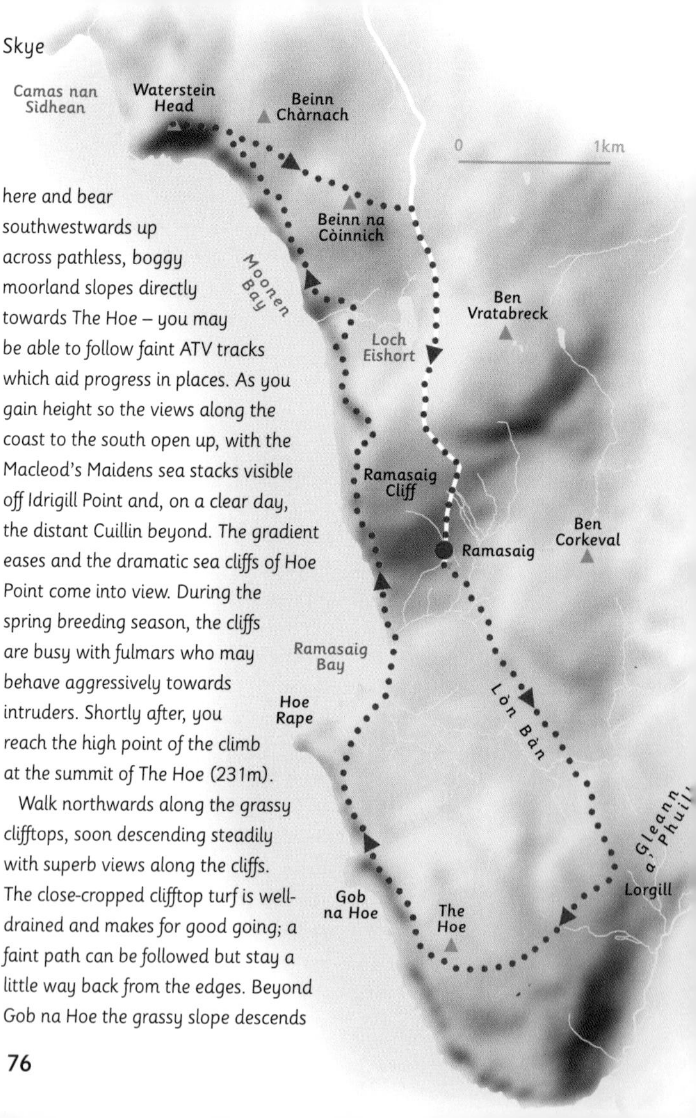

Skye

Camas nan
Sidhean

Waterstein
Head

Beinn
Chàrnach

0   1km

Beinn na
Còinnich

Moonen
Bay

Loch
Eishort

Ben
Vratabreck

here and bear
southwestwards up
across pathless, boggy
moorland slopes directly
towards The Hoe — you may
be able to follow faint ATV tracks
which aid progress in places. As you
gain height so the views along the
coast to the south open up, with the
Macleod's Maidens sea stacks visible
off Idrigill Point and, on a clear day,
the distant Cuillin beyond. The gradient
eases and the dramatic sea cliffs of Hoe
Point come into view. During the
spring breeding season, the cliffs
are busy with fulmars who may
behave aggressively towards
intruders. Shortly after, you
reach the high point of the climb
at the summit of The Hoe (231m).

Ramasaig
Cliff

Ramasaig

Ben
Corkeval

Ramasaig
Bay

Hoe
Rape

Lòn Bàn

Walk northwards along the grassy
clifftops, soon descending steadily
with superb views along the cliffs.
The close-cropped clifftop turf is well-
drained and makes for good going; a
faint path can be followed but stay a
little way back from the edges. Beyond
Gob na Hoe the grassy slope descends

Gob
na Hoe

The
Hoe

Gleann a' Phuill

Lorgill

more steeply down to the lovely little headland of Hoe Rape with tremendous views back to The Hoe, ahead to Ramasaig Cliff and across Moonen Bay to Waterstein Head and the lighthouse at Neist Point. An impressive waterfall can be seen where the Moonen Burn drops over the edge between the two great clifftops.

From Hoe Rape, begin the grassy descent to Ramasaig Bay. At the bottom of the slope, cross a ford in the burn flowing down to Ramasaig Bay and go through the stock gate in the fence ahead before bearing left to follow it along the landward side – don't be tempted to stay on the outside as the cliff edge soon becomes impassable. Continue over the undulations of old lazy beds, before coming to a second burn in 400m.

You can return to the start from here by following the burn up past the ruins of the cleared township of Ramasaig to reach the outward track by the byre passed near the beginning. Otherwise, cross the burn (you may have to cross upstream if the burn is in spate) and

follow the fenceline on the steep but straightforward ascent of Ramasaig Cliff. Partway up, a double fence runs across the route – cross this with care.

The view from the summit of Ramasaig Cliff across Moonen Bay to Waterstein Head is truly magnificent. Continue northwards, descending on the landward side of the clifftop fence, which detours slightly inland to cross the Moonen Burn – the source of the waterfall seen earlier from The Hoe and Hoe Rape, although it isn't visible from behind the fenceline here. The ground either side of the burn can be very boggy and you may have to hop across several small burns. Continue along the clifftops, soon passing Beinn na Còinnich to the landward side. Cross a fence at a junction with the clifftop fence at the head of a sheer gully, and carry on along the close-cropped turf.

Now begin the climb up the grassy flank of Waterstein Head, highest of this route's three clifftop summits and one of the tallest cliffs on Skye's coastline. The cliff edge turns sharply westwards and steepens as you climb to the summit (296m) furnished with a trig point outside the fence, which is crossed via a stile – though do so with great care. The elevated tip of Waterstein Head makes for a commanding vantage point with excellent views all around, not least down to Neist Point and back across Moonen Bay to The Hoe.

To return to Ramasaig, retrace your steps for 500m, then follow an ATV track heading southeastwards to a gate in a fence at the dip before Beinn na Còinnich. Go through the gate and keep the hill on your right, then descend on boggy ATV tracks to gain the road just beyond a cattle grid. Turn right and follow the road for 2.5km to the start.

If taking the bus, instead head NNE along the cliffs, staying landward of the stock fence for 1km before crossing via a stile at a fence junction. Continue to follow the trodden path to meet the minor road. Turn right and follow this for 1km to Milovaig road end bus stop.

Looking south to The Hoe
from Waterstein Head

Skye

Looking north from Ollisdal Geo

Duirinish Coastal Path

Distance 23km **Total ascent** 975m
Time 9 hours **Terrain** good paths along
the grassy clifftops; a couple of river
crossings could be tricky if in spate
Map OS Explorer 407 **Access** bus to
Glendale passes 5.25km from the start
of the walk at the Ramasaig road end –
and also 3.5km from the end of the walk
at Orbost road end. Parking area near
Orbost House

**The stretch of coastline between
The Hoe and Idrigill Point on the
Duirinish peninsula has been
described as the most dramatic
clifftop walk in Britain. Few who
have completed the 23km walk from
Ramasaig to Orbost would disagree.**

The scenery is never short of
sensational – a constantly changing
vista of towering cliffs, natural arches,
sea stacks, pinnacles, glens, rivers and
waterfalls that vie for your attention
along the way. As well as all the
spectacular scenery to enjoy en route,
the well-drained, springy turf along
much of the clifftops is a pleasure to
walk on.

With the possible exception of the
stretch between Idrigill Point and
Orbost you are unlikely to encounter
many other walkers along the way,
which is extraordinary given the sheer
beauty of the coastline here and the fact
that this is the Isle of Skye after all. The
'remote' feeling of this walk belies the
history of the area, which was formerly
very much a peopled landscape. The
poignant vestiges of old townships at
Ramasaig, Lorgill, Idrigill and
Brandarsaig, which were abandoned
after the 19th-century Clearances, are
testament to those former times.

This is a long and challenging walk
without practical options for shortening
the route. There is an MBA-maintained
bothy at Glen Ollisdal a bit less than
halfway along, but overnighting
obviously requires carrying the relevant
gear. As the route is linear and neither
end is served by public transport, using
two vehicles is the most practical way of
getting to and from the start and finish
of the walk. When driving to Ramasaig,
leave the A863 Dunvegan to Sligachan
road on the B884 Glendale road,

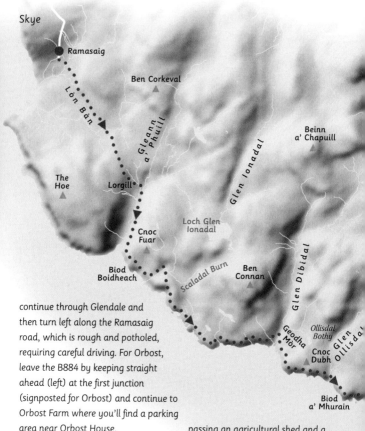

Skye

Ramasaig

Lòn Bàn

Ben Corkeval

Beinn
a' Chapuill

Gleann a' phuill

Glen Ionadal

The
Hoe

Lorgill

Cnoc
Fuar

Loch Glen
Ionadal

Biod
Boidheach

Scaladal Burn

Ben
Connan

Glen Dibidal

Geodha
Mòr

Ollisdal
Bothy

Glen Ollisdal

Cnoc
Dubh

Biod
a' Mhurain

continue through Glendale and
then turn left along the Ramasaig
road, which is rough and potholed,
requiring careful driving. For Orbost,
leave the B884 by keeping straight
ahead (left) at the first junction
(signposted for Orbost) and continue to
Orbost Farm where you'll find a parking
area near Orbost House.

Start the walk at the end of the public
road in Ramasaig – there is a stock gate
across the road here. Go through the
kissing gate next to it – with a sign for
Lorgill – and continue along the road,

passing an agricultural shed and a
sheep fank. Cross the bridge over the
Ramasaig Burn and continue along the
unsurfaced track. Pass a stone-built
byre, keep left along the main track and
continue through a gate. This part of

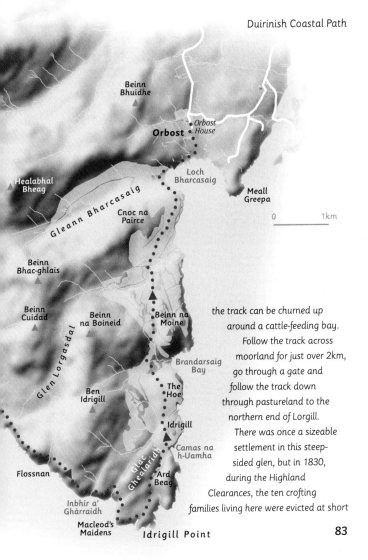

Beinn
Bhuidhe

Orbost
House

Orbost

Loch
Bharcasaig

Meall
Greepa

Healabhal
Bheag

Gleann Bharcasaig

Cnoc na
Pairce

0   1km

Beinn
Bhac-ghlais

Beinn
Cuidad

Beinn
na Boineid

Beinn na
Moine

Glen Lorgasdal

Ben
Idrigill

Brandarsaig
Bay

The
Hoe

Idrigill

Camas na
h-Uamha

the track can be churned up
around a cattle-feeding bay.
Follow the track across
moorland for just over 2km,
go through a gate and
follow the track down
through pastureland to the
northern end of Lorgill.

There was once a sizeable
settlement in this steep-
sided glen, but in 1830,
during the Highland
Clearances, the ten crofting
families living here were evicted at short

Flossnan

Glac Ghealaraidh

Ard
Beag

Inbhir a'
Gharraidh

Macleod's
Maidens

Idrigill Point

83

notice and compelled to board ship to Nova Scotia on pain of imprisonment.

Follow the track down across a small burn and through a gateway to reach the ruin of a substantial crofthouse beside the Lorgill River. Go through a gate in the boundary fence by the ruin and, unless it is in spate, you can cross the river here where the track fords it, although wet feet are likely. Otherwise you can cross the burn where it flows out across the pebble beach at the mouth of the glen. Either way, continue down through Lorgill (an ATV track continues along the eastern side of the burn), which is dotted with the ruins of blackhouses, byres and fanks, to reach the mouth of the glen.

From the beach follow a vague path climbing around the south side of the bay, steadily gaining height to reach the verdant clifftop at Biod Boidheach – the aptly named 'Beautiful Cliff'. Continue along the clifftop a short way to meet a steep-sided inlet, or geo, cutting inland. At its head a ravine carries the Scaladal Burn over a waterfall into the geo. From the edge of the geo there is a great view of a natural arch through the cliffs on the far side. Head inland alongside the geo to find a path descending into the ravine via a stepped rock ledge above the waterfall, then climb out the other side.

Continue along the springy, well-drained turf, following the cliffs high above a large bay. On approaching the next bay, there is a fantastic view down to a tunnel-like natural arch passing right through the next headland. Beyond the headland the route descends slightly and passes above a cove – one of only a few places along the route where it is possible to descend to the shore. Continue along the clifftop, soon passing around another cove; there are fine views along the coastline ahead to the distant Macleod's Maidens. After passing a third cove the trodden path joins ATV tracks, which lead steeply down through the grass and heather towards Geodha Mòr, the 'Big Channel', at the mouth of Glen Dibidal.

The Dibidal River flows through the

glen, then cascades down to the sea in a series of waterfalls. Cross the river upstream where safe to do so, then bear right and follow the trodden path back to the clifftops. It is possible to descend to the shore at Geodha Mòr through a rough gully a short way south of where the river plunges down to the sea. Continue on the path along the clifftops, which soon climbs quite steeply before levelling out, then descending a little to cross the Ollisdal River above Ollisdal Geo. The isolated metal-roofed building visible about 500m up the glen is the Ollisdal bothy, which is maintained by the Mountain Bothies Association (MBA).

Once across the burn, follow the trodden path southeast, climbing steadily along the cliff edge to the top of Biod a' Mhurain (106m). The view opens out southeastwards across Lorgasdal Bay, a spectacular stretch of coastline adorned with sea stacks, caves, natural arches, towering cliffs and a magnificent waterfall – where the Lorgasdal River tumbles down to the shore – as well as a fine view of

Macleod's Maidens standing sentinel off Idrigill Point.

Follow the clifftop path around to cross the Lorgasdal River, then continue to a gate in a stock fence. Go through and climb steadily to the high cliffs along the flank of Ben Idrigill. From the clifftop high point of Flossnan (200m), with its commanding views, the path descends into Inbhir a' Gharraidh where three burns have to be crossed, the second requiring a fairly steep descent. The path becomes a bit sketchy, but it's easy to stay on track and follow the clifftop along to Rubha na Maighdeanan. The main path doesn't continue out to the viewpoint above the Maidens, but it's a straightforward detour. The largest is known as 'the Mother' and her two smaller companions are known as 'the Daughters'.

Rejoin the main path, which soon leads northeast away from the coast. The path becomes more distinct and the character of the walk changes along with the terrain. Go through a gate and continue through the Glac Ghealaridh, a narrow valley between low hills. As you

continue above the inlet of Camas na h-Uamha, old lazy beds are visible near the remains of the cleared village of Idrigill. Continue through a deer fence and cross the Idrigill Burn. The path climbs through Rebel's Wood plantation – established in memory of punk legend Joe Strummer, whose grandmother was from Raasay – crossing the neck of a small promontory named The Hoe before descending to the Brandarsaig Burn where there are further ruins. Cross the burn flowing through a gully lined with rowan and aspen.

The path climbs again, passing through three deer fences in quick succession before crossing a low pass. Descend through rocky, heathery terrain, eventually passing through a deer fence and crossing the Forse Burn. The path becomes a forestry road that passes through a coniferous plantation on the slopes of Cnoc na Pairce before dropping down to cross the Abhainn Bharcasaig. Follow the track around the bay at the head of Loch Bharcasaig and then northwards, inland past Orbost House to reach Orbost Farm.

Looking southeast along the
magnificent cliffs beneath Ben Idrigill

Skye

Macleod's Maidens

12

Idrigill Point and Macleod's Maidens

Distance 17km **Total ascent** 590m
Time 5 hours 30 **Terrain** good paths
and track roads **Map** OS Explorer 407
Access bus to Glendale passes the
Orbost road end, 3.5km from the start.
Parking area just before Orbost House

**Standing just off Idrigill Point at
the southern end of Skye's north-
western Duirinish peninsula,
Macleod's Maidens are the island's
most impressive sea stacks, with
the highest of these jagged
monoliths rising to almost 65m.**

The route described here leads south
along the coast from the road end at
Orbost to the viewpoint on the adjacent
clifftop. This is a fine coastal walk in its
own right and it follows a clear path
most of the way to Idrigill Point.
Imaginative woodland plantation and
forestry management along the route
greatly enhances this walk, as do the
fine views along the way. It's worth
continuing northwest along the clifftops
beyond Idrigill Point if you have the time

and energy for some of the best coastal
scenery on Skye.

To reach the start at Orbost, leave the
A863 Dunvegan to Sligachan road on
the B884 Glendale road and turn left to
Orbost at the first corner to continue to
the parking area by Orbost Farm.

A signpost for Idrigill Point, Ollisdal
and Ramasaig indicates the track
leading down towards Loch Bharcasaig,
where it bends right to continue
westwards around the bay. The track
sweeps round past a house in a clearing
in the forestry and a chalet-type house
above the shingle beach, then crosses
the Abhainn Bharcasaig. Go around
a metal gate and follow the track up
into the forestry. After around 2km the
track runs out by the Forse Burn; cross
with care and continue through a
wooden gate in a deer fence. Fork right
shortly after as indicated by a marker
post. The path, which can be quite
boggy in places, climbs steadily and
eventually crosses a pass between
Beinn na Boineid and Beinn na Moine.

The path descends and leads through another gate where a sign indicates that you are now entering Rebel's Wood, a woodland plantation including birch, spruce and other native species, which was established by Future Forests in memory of Joe Strummer, frontman of anti-establishment punk rock band The Clash, who has somewhat ironically become a posthumous national treasure. Continue onwards with views over the ruined settlement of Brandarsaig to the islands in Loch Bracadale with the Cuillin dominating the horizon on a clear day. Follow the path down across the Brandarsaig Burn, flowing through a gully lined with rowan and aspen which audibly shiver with a rustling of leaves in the lightest breeze.

Continue along the path, which climbs over the neck of a small promontory named The Hoe before descending the often wet slope on the other side. Be alert to the path turning sharply right to climb again so as to avoid continuing down to a deep gorge. Cross a stream and then the Idrigill Burn shortly after, leaving the fenced woodland through another deer gate. Just beyond the burn are the stone ruins of Idrigill, once a substantial township with the undulating patchwork of many old lazy beds all around. Follow the path uphill and through the Glac Ghealaridh, a narrow valley leading up between low hills – Steineval to the right and Àrd Beag to the left. Go through another gate and continue briefly along the right-hand side of a fence before heading SSW along trodden paths to reach the coast at the sheer-sided inlet of Geodha nan Daoine. Continue out onto the narrow headland flanking the eastern (left-hand) side of the inlet.

From this vantage point there are tremendous views of Macleod's Maidens. The largest stack is 'the Mother' while the two smaller stacks are 'the Daughters'. The Mother stack was first climbed in 1959 – a daunting

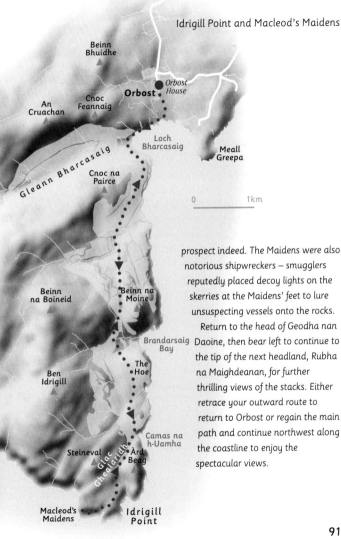

prospect indeed. The Maidens were also notorious shipwreckers – smugglers reputedly placed decoy lights on the skerries at the Maidens' feet to lure unsuspecting vessels onto the rocks.

Return to the head of Geodha nan Daoine, then bear left to continue to the tip of the next headland, Rubha na Maighdeanan, for further thrilling views of the stacks. Either retrace your outward route to return to Orbost or regain the main path and continue northwest along the coastline to enjoy the spectacular views.

Skye

Oronsay's clifftop summit

13

Oronsay Island

Distance 5km **Total ascent** 190m
Time 2 hours 30 **Terrain** good path;
the causeway connecting Oronsay to
Ullinish Point is submerged for a couple
of hours or so either side of high tide
Map OS Explorer 410 **Access** bus to
the Ullinish House hotel from Portree
(it is possible to fit the walk between
buses, should the tides align)

**The small verdant island of
Oronsay is one of a number
of islands scattered about Loch
Bracadale, but unlike its near
neighbours it has the distinct
advantage of being accessible at
low tide via a narrow causeway.**

Oronsay is a sloping green wedge of
an island, rising from Loch Bracadale to
vertical cliffs more than 70m high; it's
a joy to walk around, taking in the
expansive views and the impressive cliffs
and other coastal features, but it's also
a great spot for pausing to watch for
seals, seabirds and other wildlife.
However, it is important to check the
tide times to ensure that you cross to
Oronsay as the tide is going out, if you

want to avoid becoming stranded.
Oronsay is uninhabited and there is no
water source on the island. There is
good signage to get to the start of the
walk and the route is quite
straightforward and fairly undemanding.

If driving, take the minor road off the
A863 Sligachan to Dunvegan Road,
signposted for Ullbhinnis (Ullinish) –
there is also a sign for Ullinish Country
Lodge. After 1.5km, turn left at a
signpost for the 'Oronsay Path (tidal)'.
At the end of the road where it forks
between a few houses, there is a small
parking area on the left.

If starting from Ullinish House (which
adds a few hundred metres each way to
the route), where a signpost indicates
the 'Oronsay Path' to the left and
'Alternative Start to Oronsay Path (No
Vehicle Access)' to the right, turn right
down a narrow tarmac lane, pass a
house on the right and another on the
left, then just before the next house on
the left, turn left (a small sign indicates
'footpath') along a fenced-in path. At its
end, turn right alongside another fence
to reach a narrow tarmac lane. Turn

right, walk along the road to its end where it forks between a few houses and bear left by a small parking area.

Just beyond the parking area, there's a signpost for Oronsay via the Tidal Causeway. Go through the adjacent kissing gate, then another by a small fank and follow the old track across a field, with views opening up west and northwest to MacLeod's Tables and the islands of Loch Bracadale. At the far side of the field, the path continues through another gate in an old wall and continues around a small bay; there are good views of Tarner Island with its impressive arch to the north. The deteriorating path gently climbs the rise of Àrd nan Gamhain ahead, then crosses some boggy ground approaching another gate looking over Oronsay across the causeway below. Go through this and follow the path down through a rocky gully to the boulder-strewn shore.

There are more than 20 Oronsays, Oransays or Ornsays in the Hebrides, including two on Skye – the other being Isle Ornsay in Sleat. The name may derive from the Old Norse term for a tidal island, *Örfirisey*, meaning 'Island of the Ebb Tide'. The stones on the tidal causeway are slippery, so pick your way across with care. Once over the causeway the springy turf makes for easy going underfoot. Climb a grassy slope and bear right to follow paths along the north side of the island, making for Oronsay's high points. Continue along the path to the far end of Oronsay, detouring to visit the high points atop impressive cliffs – there is no protection against falling in the event of a slip, so keep well back from the edge. There are grand views of the other islands in Loch Bracadale and across to the north coast of Duirinish – Macleod's Maidens visible off Idrigill Point. At the furthest southwest point of the island,

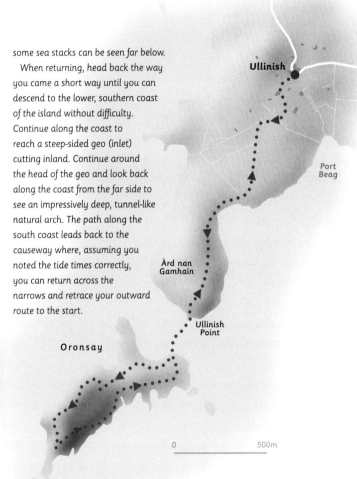

Oronsay Island

some sea stacks can be seen far below.

When returning, head back the way you came a short way until you can descend to the lower, southern coast of the island without difficulty. Continue along the coast to reach a steep-sided geo (inlet) cutting inland. Continue around the head of the geo and look back along the coast from the far side to see an impressively deep, tunnel-like natural arch. The path along the south coast leads back to the causeway where, assuming you noted the tide times correctly, you can return across the narrows and retrace your outward route to the start.

Ullinish

Port Beag

Àrd nan Gamhain

Ullinish Point

Oronsay

0   500m

Preshal Beg's basalt columns

14

Preshal Beg and Preshal More

Distance 12km **Total ascent** 695m
Time 5 hours 30 **Terrain** pathless; dense
heather and moor grass; care is needed
on cliff edges, especially in windy
conditions; good navigational skills
are essential **Map** OS Explorer 411
Access bus from Portree calls
at Carbost, 8km from the start

Lying at the end of the long single-track road through Gleann Oraid, the small settlement of Talisker has a sublime setting, a short way inland from the enchanting Talisker Bay on the west coast of the Minginish peninsula.

Talisker itself comprises a farm and a
manor house together with a few estate
residences; Talisker Distillery is actually
at Carbost on the east coast of the
peninsula. Talisker Bay is fringed with a
fine beach of sand and pebbles, which is
best visited at low tide. The northern
side of the bay is framed by sheer cliffs
and a mighty waterfall, while the
southern side is bounded by tiered
basalt cliffs and a huge sea stack. The
beach is rightly popular with visitors,
but most are content to admire the
rocky prow of Preshal More, which
looms portentiously above Talisker, from
afar. Resembling a far-flung outlier of
Sutherland's Assynt Giants, its sheer
flanks present a daunting prospect.

However, Preshal More and its sibling
Preshal Beg can, in fact, be climbed
with relative ease. Furthermore, the
best way to include both hills in a
circular walk from Talisker also involves
walking out along the highest cliffs of
the Minginish coast, rising to 280m at
mighty Biod Ruadh.

At close quarters, these unusual hills
reveal their truly outstanding feature.
Remarkable hexagonal basalt columns,
like those on the Inner Hebridean Isle
of Staffa and the Giant's Causeway in
County Antrim, swarm high up the
flanks of both hills – although Preshal
Beg has the most impressive array.
It's worth factoring extra time into your
itinerary for the moments you'll likely
spend staring in wonder and snapping
photos of these geological marvels.

Park carefully near the end of the
tarmac road to Talisker, taking care not

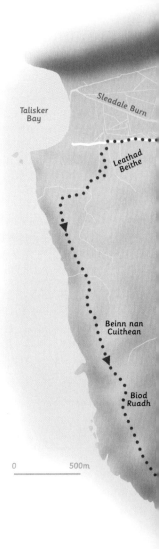

to block the turning area or any passing places – a small disused quarry on the left 300m before the road end is probably the best bet. From the road end, fork left along the track at a sign for the beach. Continue along the track, go through a gate and pass the white-painted Talisker House. The stately house was built in the 1720s and was home to the Macleods of Talisker for centuries.

Dr Samuel Johnson and James Boswell famously visited Talisker in September 1773, the latter describing it as 'a better place than one commonly finds' in Skye. He went on to detail its 'wide expanse of sea, on each hand of which are immense rocks; and, at some distance in the sea, there are three columnar rocks rising to sharp points. The billows break with prodigious force and noise on the coast of Talisker'. However, Dr Johnson, not particularly a fan of wild elemental landscapes, was less impressed: 'Talisker is the place beyond all that I have seen from which the gay and the jovial seem utterly excluded; and where the hermit might expect to grow old in meditation, without possibility of disturbance or

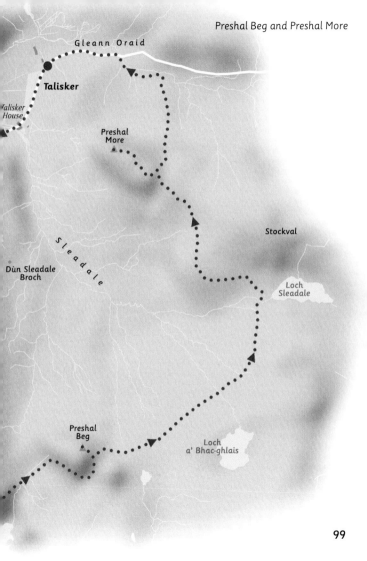

Gleann Oraid

Talisker

Talisker
House

Preshal
More

Sleadale

Dùn Sleadale
Broch

Stockval

Loch
Sleadale

Preshal
Beg

Loch
a' Bhac-ghlais

interruption. It is situated very near the sea, but upon a coast where no vessel lands but when it is driven by a tempest on the rocks. Towards the land are lofty hills streaming with waterfalls.'

Continue along the track, cross a bridge over the Sleadale Burn and go through another gate. Looking back, the prominent dome of Preshal More dominates the horizon beyond the houses. Around 750m along the track from the house, opposite a gate in the fence on the right, turn left to head up the very steep grassy slopes of Leathad Beithe. Sheep paths can be used to aid a zigzag ascent. Continue up the tiered basalt escarpment, eventually pulling yourself up over a small rocky outcrop; as you gain height, the views over Talisker Bay are tremendous.

Once the gradient eases, bear southwest across rough moorland to reach the coastal cliffs. Continue southwards as the going improves along the grassy clifftops, which rise over Beinn nan Cuithean with the mighty profile of Biod Ruadh beyond. Continuing on, the stone ruins of Dùn Sleadale Broch lie around 750m to landward. Climb steadily along the spectacular airy clifftops to reach Biod Ruadh – the highest point of the Minginish coastline – its sheer cliffs rising 280m from sea level. To the east the ground drops steeply down to a bealach at the head of a narrow glen, which runs northwards back towards Talisker. Rising beyond the bealach is the otherworldly summit of Preshal Beg; a wedge of scree-skirted rock, its flanks fluted with remarkable dolerite columns. Rather than descending to the bealach to approach the hill, it's worth continuing along the coast for a further 650m to the head of a dramatic deep inlet for stunning views.

Now head initially northwards towards the bealach to avoid boggy ground before swinging right to climb the slope to the bottom of the screes below the cliffs on Preshal Beg's south-western flank. The lower portion of the cliffs is clad with hexagonal dolerite columns like those on Staffa or the Giant's Causeway, while the screes beneath are littered with collapsed columns. These striking features were formed when hot liquid magma was forced to the surface, then shrank as it cooled, cracking in regular patterns that resulted in the distinctive hexagonal jointing. The uniformity of the lava's composition and the speed of cooling are contributory factors.

Continue around the southwest flank just below the scree, cross some rocky ground at Preshal Beg's southeast corner, then climb the obvious grassy slope to the col between Preshal Beg and the smaller rocky hill immediately to its east. From here, it's an easy detour up to the summit – a rocky plateau with the summit marked by a stone pile cairn. There are expansive views west to Rùm and Canna with the Western Isles visible on a clear day. To the north across the Sleadale moors, Preshal More lies in wait. Retrace your route to the col, then bear initially eastwards to contour along the moorland sweeping around in a curve above Sleadale.

The ground is intermittently boggy and tussocky, though the going is reasonable with sheep paths aiding progress. Make for the outflow of Loch Sleadale at its western tip, with a view of the Black Cuillin beyond. Now bear northwestwards towards the eastern end of Preshal More where a col gives easy access to the summit plateau via a grassy rake. Preshal More's summit is the high point at the eastern end of the summit plateau at the top of the climb, but it's worth heading to the cairn atop its northwestern point for the views over Talisker Bay.

To descend back to Talisker, retrace your route across the summit plateau and down the grassy rake to the col. The steep grassy gully to the north provides a route down avoiding the cliffs. Continue down the slopes to the River Talisker, then bear left to follow it down to the floor of the glen. Cross a fence and continue across the rough pastureland with the river on your right. On reaching the road just beyond a cattle grid, turn left to follow it back down to the start.

Descending the north ridge
of Beinn Dearg Mhòr with
the steep southeast flank
of Glamaig ahead

The Beinn Deargs

Distance 12.75km **Total ascent** 1255m
Time 6 hours **Terrain** mostly on paths;
steep scree slopes on higher ground
Map OS Explorer 411 or Harvey
Superwalker Skye: The Cuillin
Access bus to Sligachan from Portree,
Broadford and Kyleakin

This fine route around the Red Hills
– or Red Cuillin, as they're also
known – takes in the summits of
Beinn Dearg Mheadhonach (Middle
Red Mountain) and Beinn Dearg
Mhòr (Big Red Mountain) with the
option of including Glamaig for
those with time and energy.

Whereas the towering, jagged peaks
of the Black Cuillin are composed
mainly of basalt and gabbro, the
rounded summits of the Red Hills are
principally formed of granite, which
lends them a reddish tinge in certain
light conditions – hence the name.
These fine hills are linked by splendid
whale-backed ridges and their summits
provide some of the grandest views on

Skye – not least across the glen to the Black Cuillin.

Though smaller in scale and presenting none of the technical difficulties of their illustrious neighbours across Glen Sligachan, the scree-clad Red Hills should not be underestimated. A round of the Beinn Deargs and Glamaig makes for a challenging and exhilarating day on the hills involving 1255m of ascent and descent through some rugged terrain. Steep scree slopes can be hard work on the knees and thighs, especially up and down the flank of Glamaig. In wet or wintry conditions, the scree slopes can be treacherous.

Start by going through a gate by the old bridge on the opposite side of the River Sligachan from the hotel. Pass left of the Collie and McKenzie memorial, follow the Glen Sligachan path for 250m, then turn left through a gate to join a smaller path continuing by the Allt Daraich gorge. Cross some boggy ground, go through another gate and follow a line of old iron fenceposts. Where the posts bear left to follow the river, continue southeast on a vague path across boggy moorland; the onward path can be seen climbing the Druim na Ruaige ridge ahead to the southeast.

The ground becomes drier as you climb; a brief steep section culminates at the cairn on Sròn a' Bhealain (429m) at the northwest end of the Druim na Ruaige, with Beinn Dearg Mheadhonach and Beinn Dearg Mhòr looming ahead. The gradient eases and the broad grassy ridge makes for a gentle climb

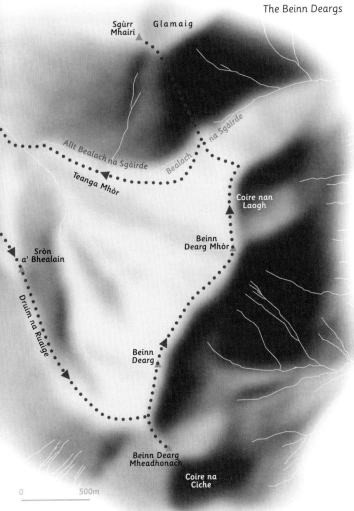

Sgùrr Mhairi

Glamaig

Allt Bealach na Sgàirde

Bealach na Sgàirde

Teanga Mhòr

Coire nan Laogh

Beinn Dearg Mhòr

Sròn a' Bhealain

Drùim na Ruaige

Beinn Dearg

Beinn Dearg Mheadhonach

Coire na Ciche

0   500m

before the path zigzags more steeply up the scree-strewn slopes to a cairn. The onward route bears NNE, but continue southeast along the ridge for 300m to the summit of Beinn Dearg Mheadhonach (651m) with views of Sgùrr nan Gillean and Sgùrr a' Bhàsteir across the glen. Return to the cairn and descend the easy slopes of the north ridge to Bealach Mosgaraidh.

From the bealach the path climbs the long steep ridge, zigzagging up through scree to the narrow summit of Beinn Dearg Mhòr (731m). From this airy vantage point, there are expansive views east along Loch Ainort to the Inner Sound. Immediately to the north are Glamaig's main summit, Sgùrr Mhairi (775m), and its lower top, An Coileach (673m). Descend gently along the north ridge for around 500m, before bearing northwest down an extremely steep slope of scree and larger stones to the Bealach na Sgàirde. The descent requires care – walking poles are very useful here. From the Bealach na Sgairde you can either

descend west right away, eventually reaching and crossing the Allt Daraich and following it back to Sligachan, or you can first tackle the daunting steep-sided dome of Glamaig rising directly above the bealach.

To ascend Glamaig, climb northwest, keeping to the left of broken rocks and making your way up the very steep grass and scree slope. The tough gradient eventually eases and the summit of Sgùrr Mhairi is just a little further northwest (left). From the summit it is possible to descend directly west to Sligachan, but this is a punishing route down a horrendous, interminable scree slope. Discounting this option, just retrace your steps from the summit down to Bealach na Sgàirde.

From the bealach descend initially southwest to pick up a path contouring around the head of the Allt Bealach na Sgàirde; gain the spur to the left of the burn, which makes for easier walking. Follow the burn down to where it meets the Allt Daraich; cross the river here and follow the left bank back to Sligachan.

Beinn Dearg Mheadhonach,
Beinn Dearg Mhòr and Glamaig
seen from Marsco

Skye

On Marsco's summit ridge
with Ruadh Stac (middle)
and Blà Bheinn beyond

Marsco

Distance 14km **Total ascent** 800m
Time 5 hours 30 **Terrain** good path
along Glen Sligachan; the north ridge is
rocky in its upper reaches; steep
descent; good path along the Allt na
Measarroch **Map** OS Explorer 411 or
Harvey Superwalker Skye: The Cuillin
Access bus to Sligachan from Portree,
Broadford and Kyleakin

**Marsco is arguably the finest of
the Red Hills — otherwise known
as the Red Cuillin — forming the
eastern flank of Glen Sligachan.
Approached from Sligachan, Marsco
is easily identifiable, standing
sentinel-like in isolation with its
elegant profile of sweeping lines
interrupted by the craggy nose of
Fiaclan Dearg — a granite outcrop
on the western flank.**

At 736m, Marsco is neither a Munro
nor a Corbett, but a Graham — those
Scottish peaks between 2000 and 2500
feet. Size isn't everything, however, and
climbing Marsco is always a worthwhile
endeavour in its own right, but it is the
breathtaking panorama of Skye's most

iconic mountains that makes it an unforgettable one.

Marsco is usually climbed from the Glen Sligachan path as an out-and-back route along the Allt na Measarroch to the Màm a' Phobuill bealach between Marsco and Beinn Dearg Mheadhonach, then along the east edge of Coire nan Laogh to the summit ridge. The circular route described here is a little more demanding, but it offers variety and enjoys the best of the spectacular views this fine mountain has to offer.

Start at Sligachan on the opposite side of the river from the hotel, by the old bridge. A signpost for Loch Coruisk, Glen Brittle, Elgol and Kilmarie points along the glen – go through the gate to join the Glen Sligachan path. Pass to the left of the Collie and Mackenzie memorial and follow the main path along Glen Sligachan, crossing several small burns. There are superb views, with the jagged summit of Sgùrr nan Gillean crowning the northern terminus of the Black Cuillin ridge to the right, the Red Hills to the left, and the distinctive profile of Marsco directly

ahead. After 3km the path reaches the Allt na Measarroch flowing down between Marsco and Beinn Dearg Mheadhonach. Cross the river and leave the path to your left. Follow the Allt na Measarroch eastwards for a short way, looking out for the best line to branch away over rough, boggy ground to gain the steep north ridge of Marsco.

Climb initially southeastwards up the ridge on grassy slopes before trending south, rising ever more steeply as the terrain becomes rockier. The gradient eventually relents and you soon gain the lower northern top. There are grand views northeast to the neighbouring Red Hills, the Beinn Deargs and Glamaig. Cross a slight dip and continue on an easier gradient to the main summit.

You reach a stone cairn just before the true summit. The view of the Black Cuillin is certainly among the finest on Skye with Sgùrr nan Gillean and the Pinnacle Ridge looking especially dramatic from this vantage point.

Continuing southeast along a vague path, the ridge narrows quite

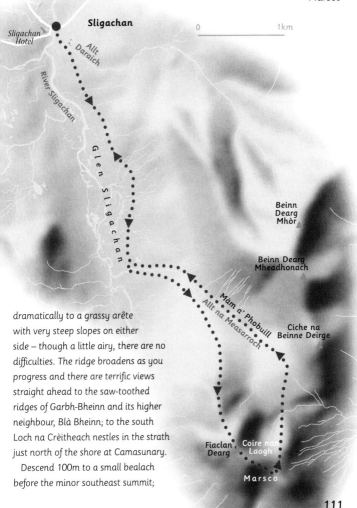

Sligachan

Sligachan
Hotel

Allt
Daraich

River Sligachan

Glen Sligachan

0   1km

Beinn
Dearg
Mhòr

Beinn Dearg
Mheadhonach

Mam a' Phobuill
Allt na Measarroch

Ciche na
Beinne Deirge

dramatically to a grassy arête
with very steep slopes on either
side – though a little airy, there are no
difficulties. The ridge broadens as you
progress and there are terrific views
straight ahead to the saw-toothed
ridges of Garbh-Bheinn and its higher
neighbour, Blà Bheinn; to the south
Loch na Crèitheach nestles in the strath
just north of the shore at Camasunary.

Descend 100m to a small bealach
before the minor southeast summit;

Fiaclan
Dearg

Coire nan
Laogh

Marsco

follow the old iron fence north down the ill-defined ridge along the eastern edge of Coire nan Laogh. Stay parallel to the fence – there is a vague path – as it makes for the bealach at Màm a' Phobuill. The fence and path cross the burn flowing out of the corrie where it drops into a deep ravine – alternatively you can cross the burn by traversing above the head of the ravine in dry conditions – and soon arrive at the bealach. From the bealach, descend northwest for 2.5km along the right-hand side of the Allt na Measarroch; there is an obvious path for much of the way, though it is eroded and very boggy in its lower reaches. Rejoin the Glen Sligachan path and retrace your outward route.

Walking along the Glen Sligachan path with Marsco ahead

Marsco

Looking east towards Sgùrr an
Fhionn-Choire, Am Bàsteir and Sgùrr
nan Gillean from the summit of
Bruach na Frithe

17

Bruach na Frithe

Distance 14km **Total ascent** 960m
Time 6 hours **Terrain** good path to start
then rocky and pathless with scree
slopes; scrambling easily avoided
Map OS Explorer 411 or Harvey
Superwalker Skye: The Cuillin
Access bus to Sligachan from Portree,
Broadford and Kyleakin

At 958m, Bruach na Frithe (Slope
of the Deer Forest) is one of 12
Munros on Skye, 11 of which are
peaks on the main ridge of the
Black Cuillin – the other being the
outlying summit of Blà Bheinn.
Of all the Black Cuillin summits,
Bruach na Frithe is perhaps the
least difficult to climb and it also
makes for one of the best vantage
points along the Cuillin Ridge.

However, this is not a walk to
underestimate as the rocky terrain
makes for rough going at times and
navigation is difficult in poor visibility.
In good conditions this is an exhilarating
walk that provides the most accessible
introduction to the daunting delights of
the Cuillin Ridge.

From the Sligachan Hotel, walk a
short way west along the old road
parallel to the A863, pass the Sligachan
Mountain Rescue Base, then at the end
of the lay-by cross the road and take the
trodden path heading away from the
road on the opposite side. Follow the
path to a footbridge crossing the Allt
Dearg Mòr (Big Red Burn), but stay on
the right bank of the river and continue
to a junction. Turn left along the track,
which leads towards Alltdearg House –
a white-painted holiday cottage. Before
reaching the cottage turn right off the
track to join the Glen Brittle path as
indicated by a sign. The path is easy to
follow as it climbs across the moor
beside the burn. To the south, the
Pinnacle Ridge of Sgùrr nan Gillean
gradually emerges from the lee of Meall
Odhair to dramatic effect.

After around 3.25km a cairn marks
the point to leave the main path to the
left and cross the Allt Mór an Fhinn
Choire burn, heading SSE. The path
climbs the grassy lower reaches of Fionn
Choire (Pale Corrie) with the peak of
Bruach na Frithe above the head of the

corrie on the right. The path is well-defined at first, but as it climbs higher and crosses the Allt an Fhionn-choire it becomes less distinct. If you lose the path, just continue the ascent bearing southeast until you reach the rockier terrain of the upper corrie where the path becomes distinct once more, climbing across rocky ground and scree on the left side of the corrie. A steep climb over a well-trodden scree slope leads to Bealach nan Lice.

The topography of Bealach nan Lice is complex and potentially confusing in poor visibility. To the left is the summit of Sgùrr a' Bhàsteir, which can also be climbed without difficulty from the bealach – the detour is worthwhile for the magnificent view of Sgùrr nan Gillean and the splendid Pinnacle Ridge. The bealach also provides a good view of an impressive rock pinnacle known as the Basteir Tooth. To the right of the pinnacle is the rocky summit of Sgùrr an Fhionn-Choire, which can be climbed by confident scramblers. To continue onto the summit of Bruach na Frithe,

follow the path through the scree below Sgùrr an Fhionn-Choire, which initially stays a little below the ridgeline to avoid some large blocks of rock before gaining the ridge and beginning the climb to the summit. The easiest route to the top stays left of the low crags. The summit of Bruach na Frithe (958m) is the only peak on the Cuillin Ridge with an OS trig point. Beyond Bruach na Frithe, the main Cuillin Ridge turns initially southwest and then southeast in a huge castellated arc – providing some of the finest mountain vistas in all of Scotland.

The easiest option for the return to Sligachan is simply to retrace your outward route. However, descending the northwest ridge makes for an entertaining alternative. This ridge is usually considered a moderate scramble, but all the difficulties it presents can be bypassed by way of a path which runs along the left side of the ridge well below the crest on scree and rough ground. The path is easier to follow when descending and avoids any

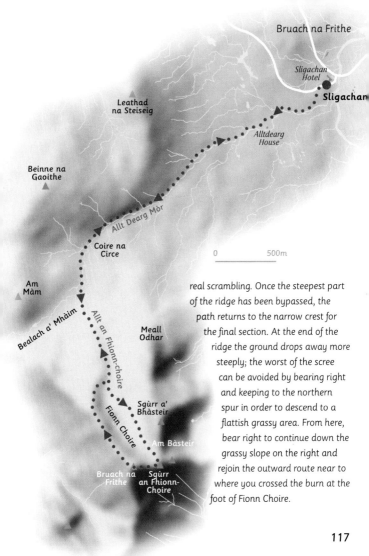

real scrambling. Once the steepest part of the ridge has been bypassed, the path returns to the narrow crest for the final section. At the end of the ridge the ground drops away more steeply; the worst of the scree can be avoided by bearing right and keeping to the northern spur in order to descend to a flattish grassy area. From here, bear right to continue down the grassy slope on the right and rejoin the outward route near to where you crossed the burn at the foot of Fionn Choire.

Climbing to the bealach between
Druim Hain and Sgurr Hain with
Glen Sligachan in the background

18

Glen Sligachan

Distance 23.3km to Loch Coruisk; 26km to Camasunary (round trips) **Total ascent** to Loch Coruisk 800m; Camasunary 390m **Time** 9 hours **Terrain** good paths; burn crossings **Map** OS Explorer 411 or Harvey Superwalker Skye: The Cuillin **Access** bus to Sligachan from Portree, Broadford and Kyleakin

Few paths in the British Isles pass through so much magnificent scenery as the Glen Sligachan path – to the east the elegant sweeping lines of the Red Hills, to the west the saw-toothed ridges of the Black Cuillin.

Unsurprisingly, the northern end of the glen by the Sligachan Hotel is often teeming with visitors, but the further along the glen you head the fewer people are encountered. A distinct path leads through the glen, although boggy ground and several river crossings can provide some challenges along the way, especially after wet weather.

A walk through Glen Sligachan presents a number of options. The

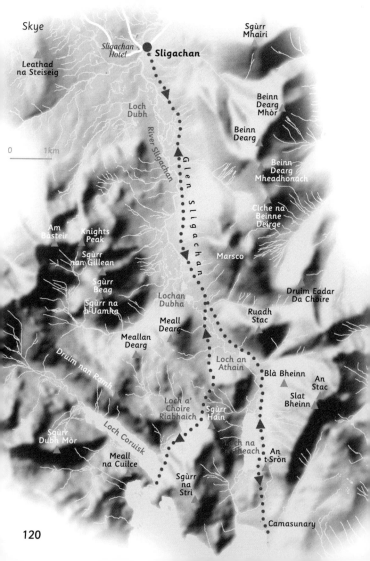

Skye

Sligachan Hotel
Sligachan

Leathad na Steiseig

Sgùrr Mhairi

Loch Dubh

River Sligachan

Glen Sligachan

Beinn Dearg Mhòr

Beinn Dearg

Beinn Dearg Mheadhonach

Ciche na Beinne Deirge

Am Bàsteir

Knights Peak

Sgùrr nan Gillean

Sgùrr Beag

Sgùrr na h-Uamha

Marsco

Druim Eadar Da Chòire

Lochan Dubha

Meall Dearg

Meallan Dearg

Ruadh Stac

Druim nan Ramh

Loch an Athain

Blà Bheinn

An Stac

Slat Bheinn

Loch a' Choire Riabhaich

Sgùrr Hain

Sgùrr Dubh Mòr

Loch Coruisk

Meall na Cuilce

Sgùrr na Strì

Loch na Creitheach

An t-Sròn

Camasunary

120

easiest of these is to walk half as far as you want to and then turn around. The alternatives include continuing on to either Loch Coruisk or Camasunary Bay, although these both make for long out-and-back routes. (In the latter case, a further alternative is to continue on to Elgol along the coast or follow the track out to Kilmarie, which requires arranging transport or coinciding with the bus service.) Both Loch Coruisk and Camasunary Bay are fine spots for camping (Camasunary also has an MBA bothy), which provides opportunities for further exploration. It is also possible to walk around the coast from Coruisk to Camasunary via the infamous Bad Step.

On the opposite side of the river from the hotel, a signpost for Loch Coruisk, Glen Brittle, Elgol and Kilmarie points along the glen – go through a gate by the old bridge to join the Glen Sligachan path. Pass to the left of the statue commemorating Professor Norman Collie and local guide John McKenzie, early pioneers in the exploration of the Cuillin. Keep to the main path, soon crossing several small burns. There are fine views of Sgùrr nan Gillean crowning the northern terminus of the Black Cuillin ridge to the right, Glamaig and Beinn Dearg Mhòr to the left and, directly ahead, the elegant form of Marsco standing proud of the other Red Hills. After 3km the path reaches the Allt na Measarroch. Cross the burn using large stones where possible – this can be difficult when it is running high. Continue along the path beneath Marsco, then after a further 3.5km you come to a fork in the path at a stone-pile cairn just beyond the pair of lochans that make up Lochan Dubha.

For Loch Coruisk

To continue to Loch Coruisk, take the right-hand branch. The path descends a little, then soon crosses a burn. The onward route can be seen climbing up towards Druim Hain; to the southeast Blà Bheinn dominates the view, its impressive west face presenting a daunting prospect. After a boggy section, the path climbs along the right side of the valley. As you gain height, the path has been bolstered by stone steps and drainage channels in recent years – the work of the John Muir Trust. The small pyramidal peak ahead is Sgùrr Hain, beyond which is Sgùrr na Strì. The gradient eases before the path reaches a large cairn atop the Druim Hain ridge. The views are splendid – Blà Bheinn looms to the east, Loch Scavaig and the southern end of Loch Coruisk are visible far below to the southwest, whilst the spires and pinnacles of the Cuillin Ridge dominate the skyline to the west.

The path forks by the cairn and the onward route to Loch Coruisk appears to be the path branching right; however, this only leads to a viewpoint, so take the left-hand branch (south) which leads to another cairn where the path forks again (the left-hand fork leads to Sgùrr na Strì). Take the right-hand fork which descends at a slant south, then southwest through Coire Riabhach with Loch a' Choire Riabhaich to your right. The path is sketchy in places and resembles a burn during wet weather, but keep heading southwest to where Loch Coruisk flows out into Loch Scavaig and you won't go far wrong.

From the shore of Loch Coruisk, the scope for further exploration is dependent on recent weather, as well as reserves of energy and daylight. There is a path all the way around the loch, but the route may be impassable if the Coruisk River at the head of the loch or the many burns flowing down from the hills are in spate. If attempting a circuit of the loch, it makes sense to go clockwise, so you will know at the start whether you can cross the stepping stones across the outflow of the loch without too much difficulty. For most mortals a loop of the loch will only be feasible if you camp overnight before the return. Retrace your outward route to return to Sligachan.

It is also possible to continue around to Camasunary from Loch Coruisk, via the infamous Bad Step. From the stepping stones across the Scavaig River follow the path southeast through the gap to emerge at the head of Loch nan Leachd. Continue along the rough path for 300m to reach the Bad Step. Descend along the obvious crack, staying low and keeping three-point contact. Once across, exhale and continue along the obvious path above the shore. The path is rough and boggy in places, but presents no further challenges until you meet the Abhainn Camas Fhionnairigh, the tidal river flowing into Camasunary Bay, after a further 3km. Find a fordable stretch up river from the old bridge – do not attempt to cross if the river is deep or fast flowing after heavy rain or when the tide is in. There are plenty of spots for camping and an MBA bothy on the eastern side of the bay. It can be busy here during the summer months.

For Camasunary

From the cairn after Lochan Dubha, stay left (straight ahead) and continue on the main path through the glen, soon crossing the Allt nam Fraoch-choire, which presents no difficulties except when in spate. The path continues past Loch an Athain and into the dramatic Srath na Crèitheach. Beneath the long south ridge of Blà Bheinn, the path passes close to the shore of Loch na Crèitheach (ignore a path branching left) before continuing to Camas

Fhionnairigh (Camasunary), one of the most enchanting corners in all of Skye. The mouth of the glen opens out into an expanse of verdant pasture running out to the wide sandy beach fringing Camasunary Bay, framed by the rugged cone of Sgùrr na Strì to the west and the south ridge of Slat Bheinn to the east. Out across Loch Scavaig the distinctive profiles of the Isles of Rùm and Eigg can be seen. There are three buildings at Camasunary – the old bothy on the western side of the bay, the substantial, private estate lodge on the eastern side and the diminutive new MBA bothy further southeast along the shore. Either retrace your steps or continue to Elgol or Kilmarie as described below.

It takes 2 hours to 2 hours 30 to walk the 6km along the coast to Elgol. From the lodge, continue southeast along the track for 250m to cross the bridge over the Abhainn nan Leac. Follow the initially boggy path south along the shore and as you begin climbing the ground improves. Cross a stile over a stock fence and carry on along the distinct though intermittently rocky,

rough and occasionally exposed path. The path is easy to follow and makes for an exhilarating walk; an airy clifftop section (care needed) precedes the descent into Glen Scaladal and, once you've crossed the Scaladal Burn, the climb out of the glen is followed by another exposed clifftop section. The path leaves the cliff edge and continues along the flank of Ben Cleat as you approach Elgol. Go through a gate onto a path between fences, then join a lane at the top of Elgol, passing a house on your left. Continue past another house to reach the road.

If you're short on time or energy, or if the weather deteriorates, then the Am Màm path between Camasunary and Kilmarie is easier and quicker (4.2km; around 1 hour 30) than the coastal route. From Camasunary, cross the bridge over the Abhainn nan Leac, then bear left to follow the ATV track that zigzags up and over the Am Màm bealach (189m) before descending for some time to the B8093 just south of Kilmarie, Kirkibost.

Looking southeastwards through
Glen Sligachan to Blà Bheinn

Skye

Loch Coruisk from the southeast

Loch Coruisk

Distance 7km **Total ascent** 150m
Time 3 hours 30 **Terrain** rough, rocky
and boggy terrain around loch shores;
rivers at the foot and head of the loch
can be impassable after heavy rain
Map OS Explorer 411 or Harvey
Superwalker Skye: The Cuillin
Access boat from Elgol (booking
required) or on foot from Sligachan;
bus to Sligachan from Portree, Broadford
and Kyleakin

There are few places that can match
Loch Coruisk for raw, rugged
grandeur. Cradled beneath the crags
and spires of the Black Cuillin, this
most impressive of all Scotland's
freshwater lochs takes its name
from the Gaelic, Coire Uisg –
approximately 'the Cauldron of
Waters'. Indeed, numerous burns
flow into the coire and the loch's
water levels can rise dramatically.

With this in mind it's fair to say that
this isn't a walk for or soon after very
wet weather. Though not an especially
long walk, the terrain is rough and
boggy in places, but while damp feet

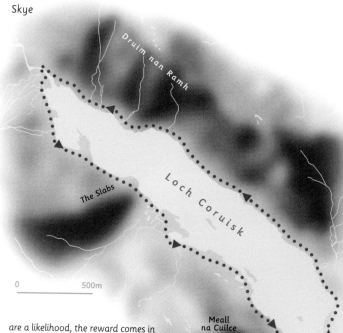

Skye

Druim nan Ramh

Loch Coruisk

The Slabs

0   500m

Meall
na Cuilce

Coruisk
Memorial
Hut

Loch na
Cuilce

Scavaig
River

stepping
stones

Eilean
Glas

are a likelihood, the reward comes in the remarkable mountain scenery along the way. If keeping to one side of the loch, the south shore is easier going and has the best views.

On foot, Loch Coruisk can be approached from Sligachan, which is a long arduous walk involving a couple of river crossings; or from Kilmarie or Elgol via Camasunary. This necessitates fording a tidal river, which can be tricky at the best of times and impossible when the tide is in or after wet weather. The route then follows a boggy path around the foot of Sgùrr na Strì, which also involves negotiating the infamous

Bad Step – a steeply-pitched convex slab of rock that drops directly into Loch nan Leachd. A crack slanting across the face of the rock provides purchase and while it's not a technically difficult obstacle it is exposed and requires good nerves. Both options are long walks that are unlikely to leave enough time to circumambulate the loch without an overnight camp – hence the more popular option of taking a scheduled boat trip from Elgol in the morning and returning with the afternoon boat trip. This also has the advantage of stunning views of the Cuillin from the sea and the possibility of spotting dolphins and porpoises.

If walking in from Sligachan, follow the instructions in the previous route for Loch Coruisk. To begin the walk from the landing stage, follow the path eastwards to the stepping stones across the River Scavaig. Cross the river, then head northeast along the Sligachan path, climbing a little before leaving the main path and heading back down towards the shore of the loch.

Continue northwest around the loch, soon crossing the outflow of the Allt a' Choire Riabhaich close to the shore or upstream – whichever is easiest. Beyond a pebble beach, the path is kept close to the shore by the steeply rising flank of Druim nan Ramh. Continue along the shore path, passing through an area of huge boulders and negotiating several rocky and boggy sections. Before you reach the head of the loch, there's a pleasant surprise in the form of a copse of rowan trees.

Otherwise known as mountain ash, the rowan is relatively common in the Highlands and Islands, where protected from grazing by terrain or deer fences. It grows at a higher altitude than any other tree in the country and can occur at close to 1000m. Rowan berries are an important source of autumn food for fruit-eating birds, including the blackbird, redstart, mistle thrush, fieldfare and waxwing. In the British Isles the rowan also has an enduring place in folklore as a tree to counter witchcraft and enchantment. The colour red was believed to be the best defence against magic and the rowan's vibrant

129

display of berries in autumn bolstered this belief. Pieces of rowan wood were carried to ward off witchcraft and sprigs were held to safeguard livestock and produce from enchantment. The rowan was once widely planted by houses as a protection against witches. Aside from its enchantment-proofing powers, the rowan is also known as the 'wayfarer's tree' as some believe it prevents those on a journey from getting lost, which might provide some reassurance if a dense mist descends on Loch Coruisk.

Cross the Coruisk River where easiest, which is usually in front of an obvious rocky outcrop with a large boulder. From atop this outcrop, there are – weather permitting – fine views of the Cuillin peaks ringing the corrie to the northwest. With its domed twin summits the central peak to the rear of the corrie is Sgùrr a' Ghreadaidh. To its north (right) are the four rugged summits of Sgùrr a' Mhadaidh. To the south (left) are Sgùrr Thormaid and Sgùrr na Banachdaich, while dominating the western side of Loch Coruisk the ridge of Sgùrr Dubh Mòr sweeps down to the loch edge. If you have time and weather on your side, it's worth continuing upstream for around 1km for fine views of Sgùrr Dearg and the Inaccessible Pinnacle, as well as Sgùrr Coire an Lochain.

Once you're done with the views, walk southeast along the shore of the loch. Areas of flat gabbro slabs with excellent grip make for easier walking, in contrast to some very boggy sections – especially towards the foot of the loch. Here, it is best to either keep close to the shore or cross the slabs above the boggy areas. Eventually, you rejoin the rocky outflow of the loch – the River Scavaig – and with it the loop of Loch Coruisk is complete.

By the Scavaig River, the outflow of Loch Coruisk

Lochan near the summit of
Sgùrr na Stri, looking to the
northern peaks of the Black Cuillin

20

Sgùrr na Strì from Sligachan

Distance 23.5km **Total ascent** 765m
Time 8 hours **Terrain** good path through
Glen Sligachan; river crossings; clear
path along Druim Hain and the flank of
Sgùrr na Strì.; vague path to the summit
Map OS Explorer 411 or Harvey
Superwalker Skye: The Cuillin
Access bus to Sligachan from Portree,
Broadford and Kyleakin

**Rising at the head of Loch Scavaig,
between the southeastern terminus
of the Cuillin Ridge and mighty
Blà Bheinn, the modest summit of
Sgùrr na Strì (494m) is dwarfed by
the sheer scale of its illustrious
neighbours. However, its position
makes for spectacular views, not
least across the mountain-ringed
sanctuary of Loch Coruisk cradled
beneath the Cuillin peaks.**

The route follows the magnificent Glen
Sligachan path south to the Lochan
Dubha, then climbs to the Druim Hain
ridge before ascending Sgùrr na Strì,
which in clear conditions provides no
great challenge. However, the summit of
Sgùrr na Strì is a complex agglomeration
of rocky outcrops and gullies, which can
be difficult to navigate in poor visibility.
Furthermore, to climb this hill in less than
good weather conditions is to miss the
point – that is the views of the Black
Cuillin rising above Loch Coruisk in all
their rugged glory.

Likewise, the overall distance of this
walk should not be underestimated. There
is a generally good path through Glen
Sligachan, though it is rocky and often
wet; indeed, after prolonged rain several
river crossings may be dangerous or
impassable without lengthy detours. It's
worth bearing in mind that any such
difficulties will need to be contended with
on the way out as well as the way in.

On the opposite side of the river from
the Sligachan Hotel, a signpost for Loch
Coruisk, Glen Brittle, Elgol and Kilmarie
points along the glen – go through a gate
by the old bridge to join the Glen
Sligachan path. Pass to the left of the
Collie and Mackenzie memorial and keep
to the main path, crossing several small
burns. There are fine views of Sgùrr nan
Gillean crowning the northern terminus of
the Black Cuillin ridge to the right,

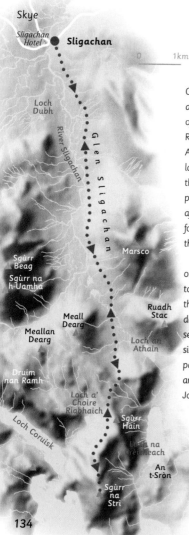

Glamaig and Beinn Dearg Mhòr to the left and, directly ahead, the distinctive profile of Marsco standing proud of the other Red Hills. After 3km the path reaches the Allt na Measarroch. Cross the burn on large stones – this can be difficult when the river is in spate. Continue along the path beneath the flank of Marsco, then after a further 3.5km take the right-hand fork at a large stone pile cairn just beyond the Lochan Dubha.

Cross a burn and continue with the onward route clearly visible climbing up towards Druim Hain; to the southeast the impressive west face of Blà Bheinn dominates the view. After a boggy section the path climbs along the right side of the valley. As you gain height, the path improves, thanks to the stone steps and drainage channels installed by the John Muir Trust.

The small pyramidal peak ahead is Sgùrr Hain, with Sgùrr na Strì lying beyond. The gradient eases before the path comes to a large cairn atop the Druim Hain ridge.

The views are splendid – Loch Scavaig and the southern end of Loch Coruisk are below to the southwest, while the spires and crenellations of the Cuillin dominate the skyline to the west.

The path forks by the cairn; take the left-hand branch (south) which leads to another cairn where the path forks again. Take the left-hand path contouring along the slopes below Sgùrr Hain. After 800m the rough path passes above a pyramidal monument known as Captain Maryon's Cairn – despite its size it can be easy to miss as it is constructed from the gabbro rock predominant on the mountain. The cairn stands nearly 3m high and marks the place where Captain Maryon's remains were found two years after he disappeared, having set off on a walk from Sligachan in July 1946. Maryon's wartime friend and fellow officer, Myles Morrison, built this fine memorial – an endeavour of considerable dedication in such a remote location.

Continue along the path for another 400m to a small burn flowing down an obvious gully. A vague path climbs by the left-hand side of the burn; follow this up to the bealach below and north of Sgùrr na Strì's summit. Turn right (southwest) across the head of the burn and climb a short way up a shallow gully to gain the summit ridge. Bear south and continue climbing, crossing large gabbro slabs on the way. The cairn-marked summit is reached soon after.

At 494m the summit of Sgùrr na Strì is half the height of the Cuillin peaks, but its situation makes it one of the best vantage points in Scotland. The seaward vista takes in Eigg, Rùm, Coll, Ardnamurchan and Mull; to the east there is a tremendous view of Camasunary with Blà Bheinn rearing up over Loch na Crèitheach. However, nothing matches the dramatic splendour of the jagged Cuillin Ridge towering above Loch Coruisk.

If you have good weather then camping near the summit is feasible and has the incentive of sunrise lighting up the Cuillin. Otherwise, retrace your outward route to Sligachan via Druim Hain.

21

Blà Bheinn (Blaven)

Distance 8km **Total ascent** 985m
Time 5 hours 30 **Terrain** good paths
but tough going; loose stones and a
scree gully; modest scrambling
Map OS Explorer 411 or Harvey
Superwalker Skye: The Cuillin
Access bus to the Blà Bheinn car park
from Broadford and Elgol

Blà Bheinn (the Blue Mountain)
is a splendid mountain. An 'outlier'
of the main Cuillin Ridge, it lacks
none of the character of its
neighbours. Its isolation only serves
to emphasise the grandeur of this
great cathedral of rock and bestows
it with fabulous views, not least of
the Black Cuillin.

Standing at 928m, Blà Bheinn is one
of Skye's 12 Munros – the only one
outwith the main Cuillin Ridge. The
ascent involves none of the difficulties
and exposure characteristic of the Black
Cuillin; nevertheless, it is a very rocky
mountain and should not be underestimated. It makes for a tough but

Blà Bheinn's eastern aspect
viewed from Loch Slapin

137

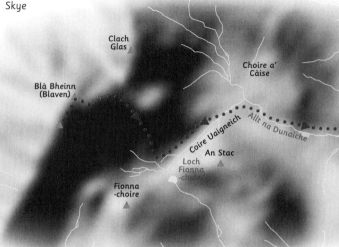

eminently satisfying climb, especially if visibility is good.

The mountain and its environs are situated on land owned and maintained by the John Muir Trust; there are toilets with a sheltered visitor information display situated in the parking area which is along a (signposted) track on the right-hand side of the road from Broadford, just beyond the bridge over the Allt na Dunaiche.

From the car park, follow the waymarked gravel path down through a deer gate to the B8083, turn left, cross the bridge and join the path on the left, which follows the Allt na Dunaiche

upstream. Initially, the path is well-defined as it climbs gently across moorland, passing through a couple of gates above the steep wooded gorge through which the burn descends. Further on, the route passes above a second gorge and around 1.75km along the route the path crosses the Allt na Dunaiche. You have to cross another burn in 300m, before the steep climb up through Coire Uaigneich begins. From here, the path becomes very stony and eroded as the towering gully-scored crags of Clach Glas and Blà Bheinn loom ever closer. On reaching the grass-floored bowl of Fionna-choire,

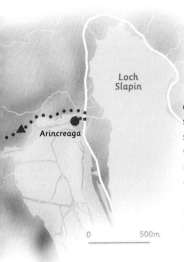

Loch
Slapin

Arincreaga

0   500m

leave the more distinct path that continues straight ahead, bearing sharply right to begin the ascent of Blà Bheinn's eastern spur. Once you've passed the cliff edges, the path becomes a little indistinct for a while as it zigzags up the steep slopes to the right.

Higher still, a faint path zigzags up across a broad scree slope. Bear slightly left, though there are tracks trending to the right, and clamber over boulders into a narrow scree gully. Continue up the steep stony gully, following the path as it bears left near the top. Thereafter, the terrain improves greatly as the route approaches the edge of Blà Bheinn's

eastern cliffs. Continue west up a slope to the left; from here, you'll have spectacular views of a vertical rock wall, part of the Great Prow. Continue upwards to a cairn with splendid views of the rocky countenance of Clach Glas.

As the climb continues, the going becomes very rocky and the upward route is channelled into a narrowing gully with a brief, easy scramble over rocks at its top; you gain the summit, with its trig point, soon after. In clear conditions, the views encompass a huge sweep of mountains, sea and islands in all directions. The panorama of the Cuillin Ridge is tremendous, as is the view along Glen Sligachan, framed by Marsco to the east and Sgùrr nan Gillean to the west.

The most straightforward way to return to the start is to retrace the outward route. It is also possible to take in Blà Bheinn's slightly lower south top, but this requires a grade 2 scramble – to do so, descend into a pronounced gap, then make the short sharp scramble to the lower top's summit.

139

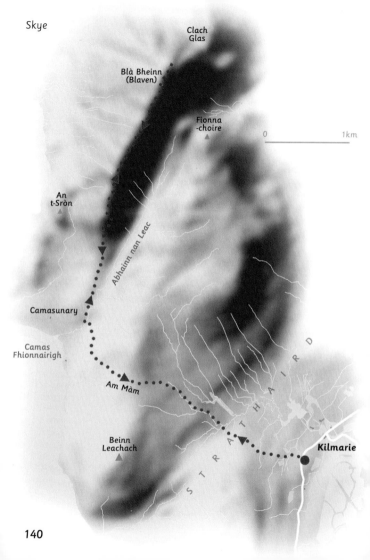

Skye

Clach
Glas

Blà Bheinn
(Blaven)

Fionna
-choire

0   1km

An
t-Sròn

Abhainn nan Leac

Camasunary

Camas
Fhionnairigh

Am Màm

S T R A T H A I R D

Beinn
Leachach

Kilmarie

140

Blà Bheinn from Kilmarie

Distance 13km **Ascent** 995m
Time 6 hours **Terrain** stony track,
rough and rocky mountain ridge and
moorland **Map** OS Explorer 411 or
Harvey Superwalker Skye: The Cuillin
Access bus to the parking area at
Kilmarie from Broadford and Elgol

**It is possible – and arguably easier
– to climb Blà Bheinn from
Camasunary, although this requires
a walk-in on the Am Màm path
from Kilmarie on the B8083
Broadford to Elgol road. The ascent
from Camasunary also takes in an
optional grade 2 scramble to reach
the slightly higher of the mountain's
twin tops (928m). There is the
possibility of camping or spending a
night in the bothy at Camasunary.**

Go through the gate opposite the
parking area to join the path, passing
a John Muir Trust information panel.
The stony track is crossed by a few
burns as you gain height, eventually
reaching the Am Màm pass after 2km or
so. Should you be blessed with good
visibility then the view across the strath

to Sgùrr na Strì and the Black Cuillin
beyond is really quite spectacular.

The path bears to the right as it
descends the flank of Am Màm, then just
before it turns sharply left for
Camasunary, leave the main path
where a pile of stones marks an initially
vague path on the right. Follow this
across a couple of burns, then cross the
Abhainn nan Leac with care. The path
becomes clearer and soon reaches a
junction. Turn right and follow the path
on up the mountain's south ridge.

As the gradient steepens to a steady
climb, the path is mostly distinct. There
are several rocky outcrops along the
ridge and these are either turned
or crossed without difficulty – small
stone-pile cairns mark the way. You gain
the slightly lower south top (926m) first
and this is separated from the higher
north top (928m) by a narrow gap.
Descending into the gap requires a
grade 2 scramble, which has to be
re-climbed on the return. Once in the
gap the north top is gained without
difficulty. Retrace the outward route to
return to Kilmarie.

The Black Cuillin across
Loch Scavaig, seen from the
Elgol to Camasunary path

22

Elgol to Camasunary

Distance 12km (round trip)
Total ascent 515m **Time** 4 hours 30
(round trip) **Terrain** rocky path; two
exposed clifftop sections
Map OS Explorer 411 **Access** bus to
Elgol from Broadford

**This fine coastal walk provides
access to Camasunary which, with
the MBA bothy and plenty of good
camping ground, makes a great
base for climbing Blà Bheinn and
exploring Loch Coruisk, lying
beneath the Black Cuillin. It also
makes an excellent out and back
walking route in its own right.**

There are fine views across to the Isle
of Rùm and the other Small Isles, as well
as along the coast to Sgùrr na Strì with
the Black Cuillin looming beyond.
Golden and white-tailed eagles can
sometimes be seen along the way.

The route starts from the right-hand
side of the B8083 in Elgol as you face
the sea (NG520139); a green Scottish
Rights of Way and Access Society sign
indicates Camasunary. Follow the
surfaced lane for 200m until tarmac
gives way to a fenced-in path between
houses. Go through a gate and continue
along the flank of Ben Cleat with a little
up and down for 1.5km before dropping
down to Cladach a' Ghlinne at the
mouth of Glen Scaladal. Cross the
greensward to the rear of the pebble
beach, step over the burn and look for
the path climbing up to the cliff at the
bottom of the flank of Beinn Leacach.
There are views of Eigg and Rùm to the
south and southwest, while to the north
Sgùrr na Strì and the Black Cuillin are
mightily impressive.

Climb up to the clifftop and go
through a gate in a stock fence. The
path continues through a tunnel of
scrubby birch and alder clinging to the
clifftop; there are a couple of airy
sections close to the cliff edge, though
these present no problems unless it is
very windy. Descending to Camasunary,
cross a stock fence using a stile; ahead
to the left by the shore is the MBA
bothy. Make for the bridge crossing the
Abhainn nan Leac 250m upstream from
the shore, then follow the track past the
lodge and across the pasture to reach

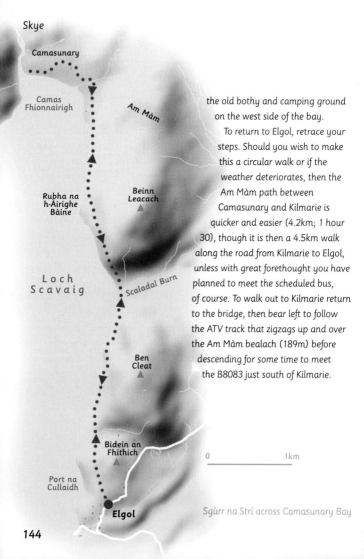

Skye

Camasunary

Camas
Fhionnairigh

Am Màm

Rubha na
h-Airighe
Bàine

Beinn
Leacach

Loch
Scavaig

Scaladal Burn

Ben
Cleat

Bidein an
Fhithich

Port na
Cullaidh

Elgol

the old bothy and camping ground
on the west side of the bay.

To return to Elgol, retrace your
steps. Should you wish to make
this a circular walk or if the
weather deteriorates, then the
Am Màm path between
Camasunary and Kilmarie is
quicker and easier (4.2km; 1 hour
30), though it is then a 4.5km walk
along the road from Kilmarie to Elgol,
unless with great forethought you have
planned to meet the scheduled bus,
of course. To walk out to Kilmarie return
to the bridge, then bear left to follow
the ATV track that zigzags up and over
the Am Màm bealach (189m) before
descending for some time to meet
the B8083 just south of Kilmarie.

0   1km

Sgùrr na Strì across Camasunary Bay

Beinn Bhuidhe and Sgùrr na Coinnich
from Bàgh Dùnan Ruadh

23

Kylerhea Hills

Distance 13.5km **Total ascent** 1230m
Time 9 hours **Terrain** rough hill and
moorland; some steep sections;
intermittent paths **Map** OS Explorer 412
Access no public transport to the start.
Parking at the Kylerhea wildlife hide
car park

**Most visitors to Kylerhea come to
watch for otters and other wildlife
from the hides looking over the
sound, or to make the short ferry
crossing of Kyle Rhea. The
horseshoe of hills rising above
Kylerhea Glen, directly across the
sound from Glenelg, continue to
be overlooked by hillwalkers drawn
to the better-known summits of
the Cuillin.**

The summits of Sgùrr na Coinnich,
Beinn na Caillich and Ben Aslak are well
separated from Skye's main ridges and
may seem unremarkable when viewed
from afar, especially in comparison with
their celebrated neighbours to the west,
but a round of all three summits makes
for an excellent day in the hills by any
standards. Furthermore, unlike almost

anywhere else on Skye, you are unlikely to encounter more than the occasional fellow walker out in these hills. By virtue of their isolation, the Kylerhea Hills also have panoramic views across Skye and the mainland mountains

This is not a walk to underestimate, however – at almost 14km long, with more than 1200m of ascent and some very steep, rough and pathless ground in places, it requires a good level of fitness. Navigation can be difficult in poor visibility, so this is a walk best saved for good conditions – all the better for soaking up the views. The hills either side of Kylerhea Glen can be walked separately by using the road running through the glen from Bealach Udal.

As you head down the road towards the Kylerhea Ferry slipway, take a turning on the left near the bottom of the hill with a wooden signpost indicating 'Wildlife Hide'. From the parking area, head straight up the steep heathery slopes of Beinn Bhuidhe. Climb steadily for some time, until the stiff gradient eases before you reach the

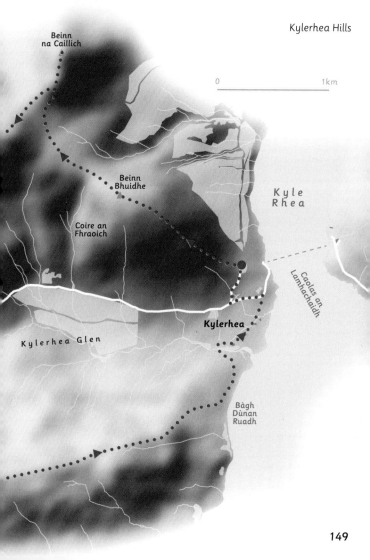

Beinn
na Caillich

0   1km

Beinn
Bhuidhe

K y l e
R h e a

Coire an
Fhraoich

Caolas an
Lamhachaidh

Kylerhea

Kylerhea Glen

Bàgh
Dùnan
Ruadh

small cairn marking the summit of Beinn Bhuidhe (488m). There are grand views eastwards across Glenelg Bay to the mountains of Kintail beyond.

From Beinn Bhuidhe, the ridge continues up towards the summit of Sgùrr na Coinnich while Beinn na Caillich rises to the right of Bealach nam Mulachag, which lies between the two peaks. As you climb Beinn na Caillich first, skirt around the eastern flank of Sgùrr na Coinnich above the Coire Buidhe, making for the bealach. From the bealach bear initially right to the eastern side of the summit, avoiding the steepest terrain, then bear left up heathery slopes, avoiding rocky outcrops to gain easier ground along the summit ridge. Faint trodden paths lead to a large stone pile cairn marking the summit of Beinn na Caillich (732m), which has fine views westwards across Skye, as well as north, east and south to the mainland mountains.

Descend back to Bealach nam Mulachag by the route of ascent, then continue up the slopes ahead. Climb initially southeastwards between rocky outcrops, trending westwards towards the summit of Sgùrr na Coinnich (739m) as the gradient eases. The summit has two cairns, one next to a trig point, and has tremendous views – especially westwards to the Cuillin.

From the summit continue southwestwards; in clear conditions it should be possible to make out the next objective – the Kylerhea road crossing Bealach Udal below. Descend southwestwards to a small lochan, then continue down the rough slopes towards the bealach, navigating a route between crags and rocky outcrops. The terrain is hard going in places with boggy ground in the lower reaches, but keep aiming for a communications mast just above the far side of the bealach and cross the Broadford to Kylerhea road here.

Follow the track up to the communications mast, then continue onto the open hillside, following an often wet trodden path. Climb southwestwards up across the eastern flank of Beinn Bheag, making for the head of a deep gully running down from the bealach on its eastern side. From the bealach, bear southeastwards up towards the summit of Ben Aslak. Pass a small lochan and as you approach the hill's craggy summit follow the right-hand of two grassy gullies leading up through the rocky outcrops to gain the top of Ben Aslak (609m), which is marked with a small stone pile cairn. Continuing an established theme, the views are excellent, taking in a vista of mountains near and far with the Small Isles seen out to the southwest beyond the Sleat peninsula.

From the summit, bear east and pass a small lochan before beginning the descent along the steadily-inclined, broad northeastern ridge leading down towards the sound at Kylerhea. The descent is straightforward for most of the way with fine views to enjoy on the way down. However, the slope does become steep, boggy and tussocky with dense bog myrtle in the lower reaches, so extra care is needed. Keep on towards the coast, aiming just to the right of a rusting corrugated shed and old drystane sheep fanks. Follow the trodden path northwards through the grass above the shore, then bear obliquely left by a small ruin and follow a path through grass and bracken to the wooded riverside. Cross a substantial wooden footbridge over the Kylerhea River, then continue on an often muddy path alongside a fence to an unsurfaced road by a house. Turn right and follow this to join the surfaced road leading out to a T-junction with the glen road, then turn left to follow it up to the right-hand turn for the wildlife hide parking area.

Skye

Woodland at Coille Dalavil

24

Gleann Meadhonach and Dalavil

Distance 12.3km **Total ascent** 220m
Time 4 hours **Terrain** good track and
path; often waterlogged near coast
Map OS Explorer 412 **Access** no public
transport to the start; buses from Portree
and Broadford stop in Kilbeg, 3km from
the start

**Unlike much of the rest of Skye,
Sleat is not famed for its walking
country and the start of this route
across moorland might confirm for
the sceptical that this position is
warranted. However, shortly after
you leave the road, the track leading
down into Gleann Meadhonach
delivers walkers to a wonderful, if
boggy, realm of wooded enclaves,
a large freshwater loch and a
coastline with views across the sea
to the Cuillin Hills.**

This peaceful landscape is also dotted
with the poignant ruins of the abandoned
township of Dalavil, cleared in the 1870s.
Most walkers will likely need longer than
the timings given here to complete the

walk as there is much to detain you
along the way and there is also scope
for exploration along the coast. The path
can be very wet in places and there are
a number of burns to cross so good
waterproof boots and gaiters are
essential for this walk.

The start of the walk is found at around
3km along the minor road from Kilbeg to
Achnacloich on an uphill stretch, where
an unsurfaced track descends to the left –
a green metal footpath sign indicates
'Ceum Dail a' Bhil – Dalavil Path'. There is
room for a couple of cars to park at the
edge of the road by the start of the track
– be careful not to block access. Head
down the track, pass around a metal
barrier and descend the path winding its
way across moorland into Gleann
Meadhonach. Go through a gate into a
deer-fenced area of regenerating mixed
deciduous woodland and native
plantation, including sessile oak, willow,
downy birch, rowan and cherry.

Continue along the track which soon
crosses and recrosses the Abhainn a'

153

Ghlinne Mheadhonaich and several tributaries. The sky-reflecting expanse of Loch a' Ghlinne comes into view ahead with the woodland of Coille Dalavil climbing the slopes above its north shore. Continue on the track, which crosses a couple more burns, and go through a gate in a deer fence. Follow the path towards the ruin of a substantial stone house with the chimney still intact, then go through a gate just beyond a large solitary tree. Continue into Coille Dalavil, designated a Site of Special Scientific Interest for its woodland, bog and fen habitats, and associated colonies of damselfly, dragonfly and lichen. Occasional waymarker posts show the way along a boggy, indistinct path towards the woodland on the north side of Loch a' Ghlinne.

Coille Dalavil is a magical place. Scots pine and beech tower over gnarly lichen-crusted birch, rowan, hazel and willow while the woodland floor is carpeted with mosses, primrose, wood anemone and wood sorrel. The woodland is alive with birdsong and in winter the loch below is home to whooper swans. The path winds its way through the lower part of the woodland, eventually emerging above the foot of the loch, where there is a channel cut by the former inhabitants of Dalavil to drain the loch and surrounding land. Pass through a tumbled drystane dyke and continue through a gate in a fence shortly afterwards, following an often very wet path through the glen towards the coast.

The path eventually leads to the ruins of the cleared village of Dalavil. The

township was cleared in the early 1870s in order for the children to receive schooling as provided for in the Education Acts of 1870-1872. Clearing the crofters was cheaper than building a school at Dalavil. The moss-covered stones of long-abandoned blackhouses date from this time, but there is also a more recently abandoned ruin that still has a few rafters and shreds of corrugated metal roof sheets.

Continue along the increasingly boggy and indistinct path that leads down to the burn and follows it out to the coastline, with the inlet of Inver Dalavil suddenly coming into view. The shoreline of the inlet is blocked by fencing near the coast. From the coastline to the north of Inver Dalavil

there are superb views northwest with the Elgol peninsula providing the foreground to Blà Bheinn and the Red Cuillin to the right and the Black Cuillin to the left rising above the island of Soay. This is also a good spot for watching seabirds going about their business and, if you're lucky, you may spot otters in the shallows or along the shoreline. There is scope for exploration northwards along the rough, pathless coast before retracing your outward route.

Loch a' Ghlinne   Gleann Meadhonach

0   500m

Looking northeast across Camas Daraich

Point of Sleat

Distance 8.5km **Total ascent** 385m
Time 3 hours 30 **Terrain** moorland; unsurfaced track and path; one moderate climb either way
Map OS Explorer 412 **Access** no public transport to the start. Parking at the road end, Aird of Sleat. Dogs must be kept on a lead

The walk from Aird out along the east coast of the Sleat peninsula to the automatic lighthouse at the southernmost point of the Isle of Skye benefits from some fine coastal scenery and excellent views – especially southwestwards to the Isles of Eigg and Rùm. The route is quite straightforward and the terrain presents no real difficulties – a firm farm track takes you over halfway, followed by a distinct if occasionally boggy trodden path for the remainder.

A minor detour leads to the sheltered bay at Camas Daraich, which is fringed by one of the finest of Skye's few sandy beaches. The point itself is a great place for spotting seabirds, including dive-bombing gannets, as well as dolphins and other sea mammals.

From the parking area at the road end, go through the wooden gate next to the stock gate – a green sign indicates the Point of Sleat – and follow the metalled track, which soon begins to wind its way steadily uphill. The track continues its sinuous course across the heather-clad moorland and as you gain height there are great views eastwards looking back across the Aird of Sleat to the mountains of Knoydart beyond. Follow the track up across the southern flank of Sgurran Seilich, with the sheer basalt cliffs of the Isle of Eigg suddenly appearing to the southwest.

Cross the high point, descend steeply and go through a gate. The track continues westwards alongside the burn flowing down from Loch Aruisg. A couple of houses come into view on the coast ahead, then just after crossing a wooden bridge next to a ford turn left to join a rocky path, signposted for the Point of Sleat and Sandy Bay. The path steeply climbs a brief rocky section beneath a gnarled sessile oak tree, then bears left

157

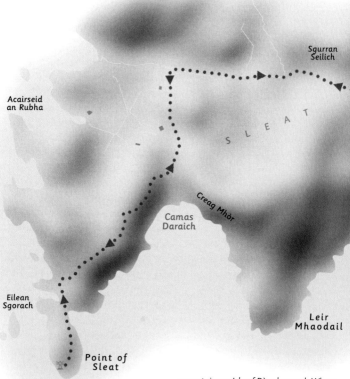

Sgurran
Seilich

Acairseid
an Rubha

S L E A T

Creag Mhòr

Camas
Daraich

Leir
Mhaodail

Eilean
Sgorach

Point of
Sleat

alongside a fence across broken, slabby sandstone and potentially boggy moorland for around 500m. To the right there are a few scattered, isolated houses foregrounding the view across to the

mountainous Isle of Rùm beyond. Where the fence makes a 90° turn to the west, continue straight ahead a short way on the rough path to reach a path junction. Bear right as indicated by a Scotways marker post to continue to the Point of Sleat, but beforehand it is worth making

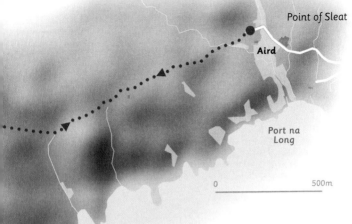

Point of Sleat

Aird

Port na
Long

0   500m

the short detour straight ahead to the beautiful sandy bay at Camas Daraich.

Having enjoyed the beach, return to the path junction and carry on heading westwards (left), following a continuous rough path as it climbs and then crosses heathery moorland, which is boggy in places, with superb views back across Camas Daraich. Eventually, narrow concrete steps (hazardous in wet conditions) lead steeply down into a broad gap. From the foot of the steps, continue straight ahead (right) towards the rocky shoreline over potentially boggy ground, then bear left and continue across a lovely strip of greensward to reach two bays, the left-hand one featuring a small sandy beach.

From here, it is just a short distance on a clear path up and over a final rise, then across close-cropped grass to reach the automatic lighthouse at Skye's southernmost point. The views from the lighthouse take in Mallaig to the east, the Ardnamurchan peninsula to the south, the isles of Eigg and Rùm to the south-west and west, and Rubha an Dùnain to the northwest beyond the Isle of Soay. The lighthouse is also a good vantage point for spotting dolphins and seabirds, including gannets and cormorants. The return is via the outward route with more views to enjoy along the way.

Index